Damaris Deschner
Frankfurter Strasse 182
34134 Kassel
Germany

Casey C.M. Mathewson

I NEUE ARCHITEKTUR AM WASSER
I NEW ARCHITECTURE AT WATER'S EDGE
I NOUVELLE ARCHITECTURE AU BORD DE L'EAU
I ARQUITECTURA NUEVA JUNTO AL AGUA

BEACH HOUSES

®FEIERABEND

Bay of Islands House, New Zealand
Pete Bossley Architects Ltd, 1999, page 112

Beach Houses

Contents
Inhalt
Sommaire
Contenido

© 2006 Feierabend Verlag OHG
Mommsenstraße 43, D-10629 Berlin

Editor, Author of English and German Texts,
Layout, Typesetting & Picture Editing:
mab - Casey C.M. Mathewson, Berlin
www.ma-b.net
Translations into French and Spanish:
Allround Fremdsprachen GmbH, Berlin
Lithography: www.artwork-factory.com

Idea and Concept: Peter Feierabend, Casey C.M. Mathewson

Printed in the EU

ISBN 3-89985-167-6
40-02043-1

Foreword

The water of which we largely consist also protectively covers most of the earth's surface and thus radiates universal power and archaic fascination. Discoverers and writers such as Rudyard Kipling have long sought to understand this phenomenon. Kipling defined his "Seven Seas" as the late 19th century's answer to Antiquity's legendary "Seven Wonders of the World". Even today, discoverers put themselves at massive risk to gain a better understanding of the secrets of the oceans.

Building on water's edge has always confronted architects with the challenge of creating more than mere shelter from harsh weather and unforeseeable natural elements. The objective here is to fully open the houses to nature and to thus achieve a dramatic unity of architecture with the natural while at the same time providing protection from catastrophic events such as bush fires, tsunamis, earthquakes, or flooding.

Finding creative solutions to this seemingly unsolvable paradox ultimately lies in the hands of architects. This book shows that there are no national or philosophical borders limiting creativity when it comes to solving this age-old building task. What unites the homes presented here with the support of avant-garde architects and photographers in Argentina, Australia, Brazil, Chile, Finland, France, Germany, Japan, Canada, New Zealand, Peru, Portugal, Spain, and the United States? The commonality in the works presented lays most certainly in their commitment to fulfilling a universal desire inherent in all mankind: to live at one with nature. This book gives insight into the broad spectrum of design responses to make this dream come true that are being explored internationally. It also provides valuable impetus for your personal, inner beach at home - however far it may be from the sound of waves breaching the ocean shore.

Point House, Montana, USA
Bohlin Cywinski Jackson, 2002, page 154

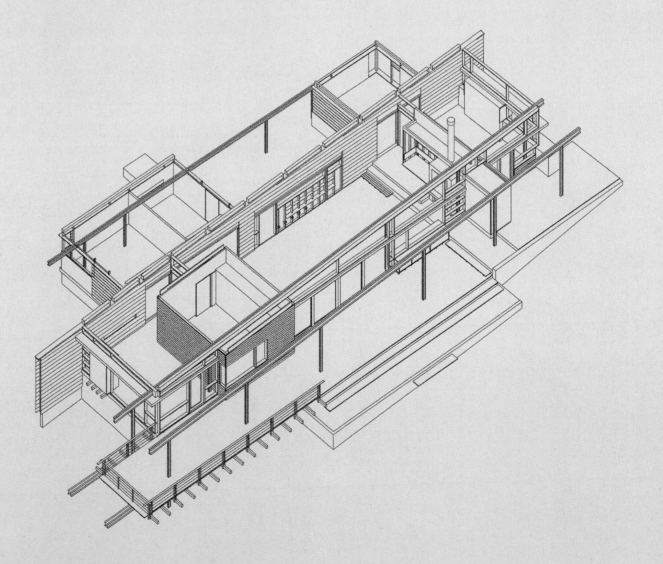

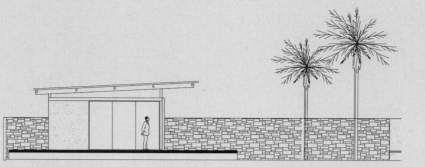

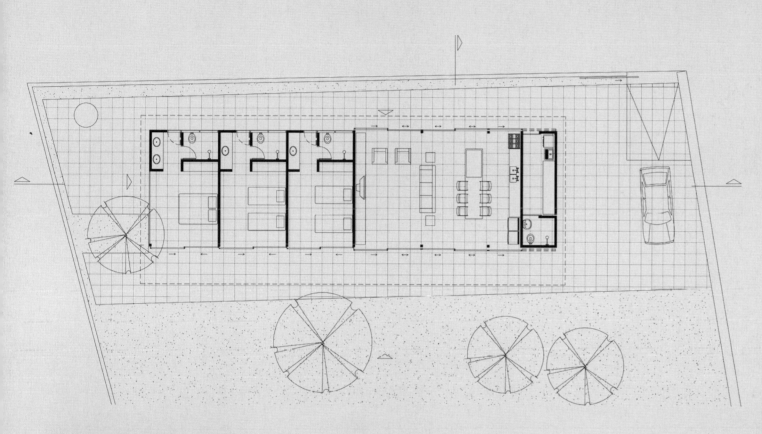

Casa in Barra do Sahy, Brazil
Lua Nitsche, 2002, page 18

Vorwort

Das Wasser, aus dem wir zu großen Teilen bestehen und das unseren Planeten schützend bedeckt, strahlt universelle Kraft und archaische Faszination aus.

Entdecker und Schriftsteller wie Rudyard Kipling haben seit jeher versucht, diesem Phänomen näher zu kommen. Kipling umriss seine „Sieben Weltmeere" als das Gegenstück des späten 19. Jahrhunderts zu den viel besungenen „sieben Weltwundern" der Antike. Noch heute setzen sich Entdecker massiven Gefahren aus, um die Geheimnisse der Meere zu erkunden.

Schon immer konfrontiert das Bauen am Wasser die Architekten mit der Herausforderung, in der schwer berechenbaren, den natürlichen Elementen ausgesetzten Lage mehr als nur Obdach zu schaffen. Denn hier gilt es, sich gleichzeitig der Natur zu öffnen und die Architektur mit dieser zu vereinen, aber auch vorbeugend gegen Naturkatastrophen wie Waldbrände, Tsunamis, Erdbeben oder Überflutungen zu planen.

Die kreative Lösung dieses scheinbaren Gegensatzes obliegt dem Einfallsreichtum der Architekten. Dieser Kreativität werden keine Grenzen gesetzt, weder nationale noch gedankliche.

Was vereint diese Häuser, die wir dank der tatkräftigen Unterstützung von Architekten und Fotografen aus Argentinien, Australien, Brasilien, Chile, Finnland, Frankreich, Japan, Kanada, Neuseeland, Peru, Portugal, Spanien und den Vereinigten Staaten präsentieren dürfen?

Es ist wohl ihre gemeinsame Beschäftigung mit der universellen Sehnsucht von uns allen, im Einklang mit der Natur beheimatet zu sein. Dieser Band zeigt, auf welch vielfältige Weise dieser Traum Wirklichkeit werden kann und liefert darüber hinaus Impulse auch für den persönlichen, inneren Strand zu Hause, auch wenn dieser weitab der Mächtigkeit von brandenden Meereswellen liegt.

Préface

L'eau, dont nous sommes en grande partie composés, et qui protège notre planète, a toujours été symbole de puissance et de fascination.
De tout temps, les explorateurs et les écrivains comme Rudyard Kipling ont tenté de comprendre ce phénomène. Kipling a notamment défini ses « sept mers » comme la réponse de la fin du 19ème siècle aux légendaires « sept merveilles du monde » de l'Antiquité. Aujourd'hui encore, de nombreux explorateurs s'exposent à de grands dangers pour découvrir le secret des océans.
Depuis toujours, la construction en bordure d'eau confronte les architectes à la difficile tâche de créer plus qu'un simple abri tout en tenant compte des conditions climatiques extrêmes et des éléments naturels imprévisibles. Car il s'agit là, non seulement de s'ouvrir à la nature en créant une architecture harmonieuse, mais également de se protéger des catastrophes naturelles : feux de forêt, tsunamis, tremblements de terre ou inondations.
Trouver une solution créative à ce qui semble être un paradoxe, voilà le devoir qui incombe à l'imagination des architectes. Une créativité sans limites, qu'elles soient géographiques ou spirituelles.
Quel est le point commun des maisons que nous vous présentons ici, grâce au soutien des architectes et des photographes d'Argentine, d'Australie, du Brésil, du Chili, de Finlande, de France, d'Allemagne, du Japon, du Canada, de Nouvelle-Zélande, du Pérou, du Portugal, d'Espagne et des Etats-Unis ?
C'est certainement la nostalgie de leurs occupants, comme celle de nous tous, de retrouver un habitat en parfait accord avec la nature.
Ce livre montre de quelles manières le rêve peut devenir réalité. Par ailleurs, il crée l'envie de réaliser, en soi et chez soi, sa propre plage intérieure, même si celle-ci se trouve loin du tumulte des vagues déferlantes.

Coromandel Bach House, New Zealand
Crosson Clarke Architects, 2003, page 54

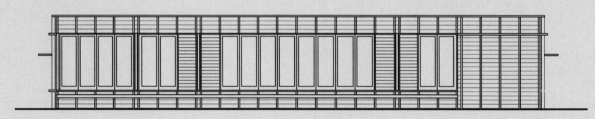

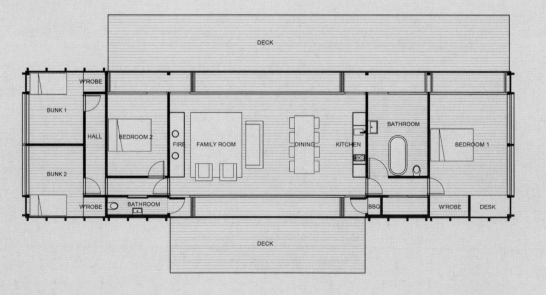

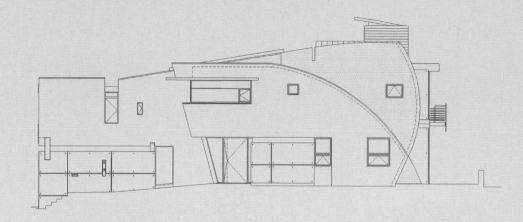

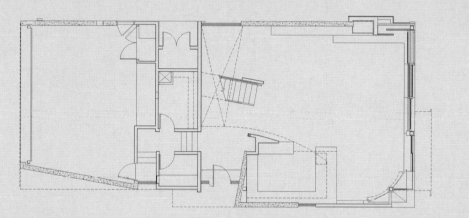

Knight Residence, Newport Beach, CA, USA
Abramson Teiger, 2003, page 116

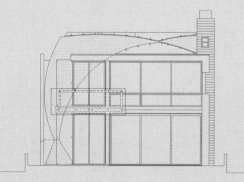

Prólogo

El agua, de la que consistimos en gran parte
y que forma un manto protector alrededor
de nuestro planeta, irradia fuerza universal y
fascinación arcaica.

Descubridores y escritores como Rudyard
Kipling siempre han intentado comprender este
fenómeno. Kipling definió sus "Siete Océanos"
como una respuesta del tardío siglo XIX a las
legendarias "Siete Maravillas del Mundo" de
la Antigüedad. Aun hoy, los descubridores se
exponen a inmensos peligros para explorar los
secretos de los mares.

Desde siempre, el construir junto al agua
ha confrontado a los arquitectos con el reto
de crear algo más que sólo un techo como
protección contra las inclemencias del tiempo
y los impredecibles elementos naturales. Aquí,
el objetivo consiste en abrirse a la naturaleza
y unirla con la arquitectura, pero planificando
al mismo tiempo en prevención de catástrofes
naturales como incendios forestales, tsunamis,
terremotos o inundaciones.

La solución creativa de esta aparente
contradicción depende de la riqueza de ideas
de los arquitectos. Para esta creatividad no hay
fronteras, ni en los mapas ni en el pensamiento.
¿Qué es lo que une estas casas, que podemos
presentar aquí gracias a la activa colaboración de
arquitectos y fotógrafos de Argentina, Australia,
Brasil, Canadá, Chile, España, EE.UU., Finlandia,
Francia, Japón, Nueva Zelanda, Perú y Portugal?
Posiblemente sea el hecho de que compartan ese
anhelo universal que hay en todos nosotros de
vivir en armonía con la naturaleza.

Este tomo nos muestra la pluralidad de formas
en que podemos realizar este sueño y además
nos ofrece impulsos para crear nuestra propia
playa interior en casa, aun cuando la misma
se encuentre lejos del potente rugir del oleaje
marino.

Casa Felix, Ubatuba, Brazil
Anne Marie Sumner, 1999, page 30

Atlantic Houses

Am Atlantik I Sur la côte Atlantique I Junto al Atlántico

Kustavi, Finland
Kimmo Köpilä & Topi Laaksonen
2005, 95 m²

On the Baltic Coast
Villa Nina
The gently sloping site dominated by coniferous trees borders on Seksmiilari Bay where it connects with the open Baltic Sea beyond. The floor plan is organized to create diverse protected outdoor spaces such as a sheltered atrium, a roofed outdoor dining area, and a terrace that can be used in even the harsh Nordic winters. The family enjoys spending time in the kitchen, but their favorite place is around the dining table. These spaces form the heart of the home. The living areas are organized to face the sunset, while the bedrooms are located in a separate wing oriented toward the morning sun.

An der Ostseeküste
Villa Nina
Das zum Meer hin abfallende Waldgrundstück liegt direkt am Seksmiilari Ufer mit Blick zur offenen Ostsee. Der U-förmige Grundriss definiert geschützte Außenbereiche wie ein Atriumhof, ein überdachter Essplatz und eine Terrasse, die auch im harschen nordischen Winter benutzt werden.
Die Familie hält sich zwar gerne in der Küche auf, aber der Esstisch ist ihr Lieblingsort. Zusammen bilden diese Räume das Herz des Hauses. Die Wohnbereiche orientieren sich nach Westen zum Sonnenuntergang hin. Schlafbereiche befinden sich in einem separaten Flügel mit Ostorientierung.

Sur la côte Baltique
Villa Nina
Le terrain boisé descend en pente douce vers les rives du Seksmiilari et s'ouvre sur la mer Baltique. Les plans de la construction, en forme de U, ont donné naissance à plusieurs zones extérieures protégées, comme un atrium, un coin-repas couvert et une terrasse, agréables malgré la rigueur des hivers nordiques.
La famille aura plaisir à séjourner dans la cuisine, mais elle préfèrera la convivialité de la salle à manger. A elles deux, ces pièces constituent le cœur de la maison. Les espaces à vivre sont orientés plein ouest, en direction du soleil couchant. Les chambres sont quant à elles situées dans une aile séparée et donnent à l'est.

Costa del Mar Báltico
Villa Nina
El terreno boscoso, en declive hacia el mar, está ubicado a orillas del Seksmiilari, con vista hacia el Mar Báltico.
La planta en forma de U define áreas exteriores protegidas, una zona de comedor techada y una terraza que también se pueden usar en el crudo invierno del norte. Además de la cocina, el lugar preferido de la familia es la mesa del comedor. Estos dos ambientes juntos forman el corazón de la casa. Las áreas de habitación están orientadas hacia el oeste, hacia la puesta del sol. Las áreas de dormitorio se encuentran ubicadas en un ala separada con orientación al este.

Simply Elegant
Juquehy Beach House

This beachside home is an exercise in simplicity and efficient use of available resources. Constructed by local residents utilizing vernacular techniques, it reinterprets Brazilian building traditions. A framework of wood trusses forms an elegant skeleton supporting the exposed roof tiles. Rising upward toward the southeast elevation, the roof defines a spacious living/dining hall and extends outside to cover the wooden deck. The bedrooms, each with deck access, are enclosed in bright blue walls. A service zone with bathrooms and the open kitchen forms a buffer on the northern street elevation.

Einfach Elegant
Juquehy Strandhaus

Das Konzept dieses Strandhauses beruht auf Einfachheit und schonendem Umgang mit vorhandenen Ressourcen. Erbaut in lokal typischer Bauweise interpretiert das Haus brasilianische Traditionen neu. Rahmen aus Holz bilden ein elegantes Gerippe, auf dem die sichtbaren Dachziegel lagern. Nach Südosten ansteigend definiert das Dach einen geräumigen Wohn-/ Essbereich und setzt sich im Freien über dem Holzdeck fort. Die Schlafzimmer sind von strahlend blauen Wänden umfasst. Die Servicezone mit Bädern und der offenen Küche erstreckt sich entlang der Nordseite.

Simple élégance
Juquehy Strandhaus

Cette résidence de plage est un exercice de simplicité et d'utilisation efficace des ressources disponibles. Édifiée par des résidents locaux utilisant des techniques courantes, elle réinterprète des traditions de construction brésiliennes. Une structure de poteaux et de poutres forme un élégant squelette qui supporte un toit de tuiles. Se relevant vers le sud-est, le toit définit un spacieux volume destiné au séjour/ salle à manger et s'étend à l'extérieur pour abriter une terrasse recouverte d'un plancher. Les chambres auxquelles on accède depuis la terrasse sont closes de murs bleu vif. Un espace technique comprenant les salles d'eau et la cuisine ouverte isole de la rue sur le côté nord.

Simplemente elegante

Casa Juquehy Beach

El concepto de esta casa situada al lado de la playa se basa en la sencillez y en el empleo eficiente de los recursos disponibles. Construida siguiendo el estilo local, la vivienda reinterpreta las tradiciones brasileñas. Una estructura de madera forma un elegante esqueleto sobre el que reposan las tejas expuestas del tejado. Éste, que se eleva hacia el sureste, define un amplio salón comedor y se extiende hacia afuera sobre la cubierta de madera. Los dormitorios están rodeadas por luminosas paredes azules. La zona de servicio con los baños y la cocina abierta se extiende a lo largo del lado norte.

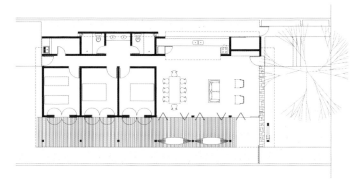

São Sebastião, Brazil, Alvaro Puntoni Arquiteto, 2001, 108 m²

Barra do Sahy, Brazil
Lua Nitsche Arquitetos Associados
2002, 130 m²

Simple, not plain

Weekend Home in Barra do Sahy

The architects developed a house form that employs simple means to effectively react to the extreme high levels of humidity and high temperatures that prevail in this region. The floor slab was elevated above site and the roof was raised over the internal volume to allow cooling air currents to flow unimpeded around the building core. Interior hallways were eliminated as continuous decks on both sides of the house serve as terraces and circulation spines. Large sliding glass wall elements can be opened to achieve a seamless merge between indoor and outdoor spaces.

Einfach, nicht simpel

Wochenendhaus in Barra do Sahy

Weitab der Schwüle der Millionenstadt São Paulo entwickelten die Architekten eine Hausform, die mit einfachen Mitteln konsequent der extrem hohen Luftfeuchtigkeit und den hohen Temperaturen der Region gerecht wird. Die Bodenplatte wurde vom Erdreich gelöst und das Dach wurde angehoben, damit kühlende Luftströme ungehindert zirkulieren können. Auf innenliegende Flure wurde verzichtet, durchgehende Decks an beiden Hausseiten fungieren zugleich als Terrasse und Flur im Freien. Große Glasschiebeelemente erlauben das komplette Öffnen der Wohnräume und schaffen einen nahtlosen Übergang zwischen Innen und Außen.

Simple, mais pas banal

Maison de week-end à Barra do Sahy

Loin de la chaleur étouffante de la métropole São Paulo, les architectes ont su, avec des moyens simples, concevoir une maison adaptée à l'humidité extrême et aux températures élevées de la région. Le plancher a été surélevé par rapport au sol et le toit rehaussé, afin que l'air puisse circuler librement.
Pas besoin de couloirs intérieurs : les pontons continus des deux côtés de la maison servent à la fois de terrasse et de couloir à ciel ouvert. De grandes baies vitrées coulissantes permettent d'ouvrir entièrement les pièces à vivre, de sorte qu'intérieur et extérieur ne forment plus qu'un.

Sencilla, no simple

Casa en Barra do Sahy

Lejos del sofocante calor de la metrópoli de São Paulo, los arquitectos desarrollaron una forma de casa que con medios sencillos reacciona a las condiciones extremas de humedad y temperatura de la región. La placa del piso se separó de la tierra y el techo se levantó para que las refrescantes corrientes de aire pudieran circular libremente. Se omitieron corredores internos, ya que las cubiertas que rodean la casa funcionan al mismo tiempo como corredor y terraza al aire libre. Los grandes elementos corredizos de vidrio permiten abrir las habitaciones completamente.

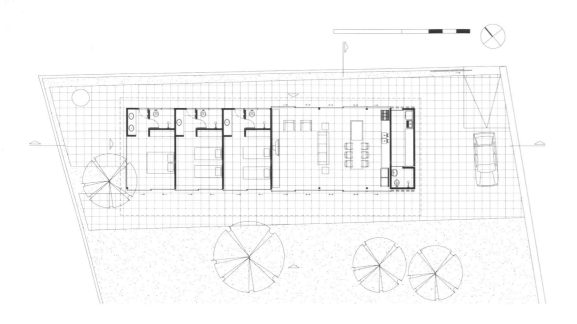

Slanting Box
At Home in the Dunes

This house's organization reacts precisely to the given qualities of the site with its dune-like topography. A private wing of rooms with bedrooms and bathrooms was embedded into the dune landscape. The gently slanting glazed box form of the living space rises above this plinth and opens to the sea beyond. This creative deployment of functions in two wings minimizes environmental impact. Walkers on the nearby beach scarcely notice the house and the inhabitants enjoy an especially close interconnection to the natural surroundings. In-situ concrete, slate, marble, wood, steel, and glass form a palette of materials that harmonizes well with the natural surroundings.

Schräge Kiste
Zuhause in den Dünen

Die Organisation des Hauses geht präzise auf die Gegebenheiten des Ortes und die dünenartige Topographie ein. Der private Flügel mit Schlaf- und Badezimmern wurde in die Dünenlandschaft eingebettet. Darüber erhebt sich die schräg ansteigende, sich zum Meer hin öffnende Glaskiste des Wohnbereiches. Der Eingriff in die Natur wird durch diesen kreativen Umgang mit den Gebäudemassen minimiert. So bemerken Strandgänger das Haus kaum und die Bewohner leben in dichter Nähe zum umliegenden Naturraum. Sichtbeton, Schiefer, Marmor, Holz, Stahl und Glas bilden eine Materialienpalette, die in Harmonie zur umliegenden Landschaft steht.

Un caisson oblique

Se sentir chez soi dans les dunes

L'aménagement de cette maison répond parfaitement aux contraintes du lieu et à la topographie propre aux dunes. L'aile privée, qui comprend les chambres à coucher et les salles de bains, a été enclavée dans le paysage de dunes. Au-dessus s'élève un caisson de verre oblique comprenant l'espace à vivre, ouvert sur la mer. Les dimensions créatives de la construction respectent la nature au maximum. Ainsi, les personnes qui se rendent à la plage remarquent à peine la maison, et ses habitants y résident en symbiose avec l'environnement. Béton apparent, ardoise, marbre, bois, acier et verre forment une palette harmonieuse de matériaux qui se marie au paysage voisin.

Caja oblicua

Vivir en las dunas

La organización de la casa se adapta a las circunstancias del lugar y la topografía de las dunas. El ala privada con los dormitorios y cuartos de baño se emplazó en el paisaje de dunas. Encima se levantó la caja de vidrio oblicua, abierta hacia el mar, que constituye la zona de estar. La intervención en la naturaleza se minimiza con este manejo creativo de las masas de edificación. Así, quienes pasean por la playa apenas se dan cuenta de su presencia, mientras que sus habitantes viven próximos a la naturaleza circundante. Hormigón liso, pizarra, mármol, madera, acero y vidrio constituyen la gama de materiales usados en armonía con el paisaje circundante.

Ofir, Portugal, José Fernando Gonçalves, Cristina Guedes, 2003, 180 m²

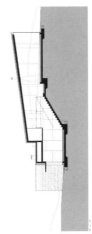

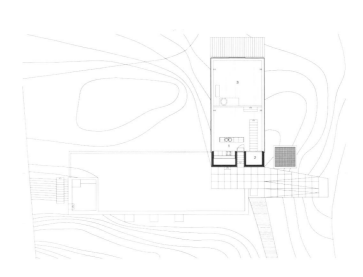

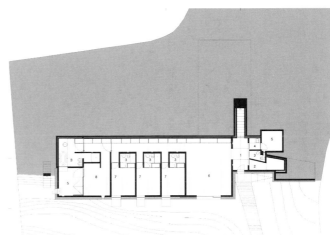

Longboat Key, FL, USA
Guy Peterson / OFA Inc.
2003, 450 m²

Ocean Boulevard

Urbanity at the Beach

The three-level design creates a solid ‚wall' behind a palm forecourt toward the busy road and opens with large glazed walls toward the sea. The ground floor contains the entry, internal reflecting pools, the garage, exercise room, and swimming pool. The pool is located on the south side of the structure for full sun and designed into the ‚base' of the house. On the first level, the living, dining and kitchen areas look out over a large covered terrace to the Gulf of Mexico. The master bedroom and owner's study are on the top floor and have private terraces that enjoy panoramic views.

Ocean Boulevard

Urbanität am Strand

Das dreigeschossige Haus formt eine solide „Wand" zum mit Palmen bestandenen Vorplatz und öffnet sich über großzügige Glasfronten zur Meerseite hin. Das Erdgeschoss beherbergt den Eingang, reflektierende Pools, die Garage, den Fitness Raum und den Pool. Dieser wurde an die Südseite des Hauses gerückt, um so die günstige Besonnung optimal auszunutzen. Wohnen, Essen und Kochen findet im 1. OG mit Ausblick auf den Golf von Mexiko statt. Das große Schlafzimmer und die Bibliothek wurden in der obersten Etage untergebracht, Sie verfügen über private Terrassen und Panoramaausblicke.

Ocean Boulevard

Urbanität am Strand

Cette maison de trois étages se dresse majestueusement sur une place ornée de palmiers, et s'ouvre sur la mer grâce à de larges baies vitrées. Le rez-de-chaussée se compose d'une entrée, de bassins d'eau miroitante, du garage, de la salle de gymnastique et de la piscine. Cette dernière a été située du côté sud de la maison, afin de bénéficier d'un ensoleillement maximal. Le premier étage abrite la pièce à vivre, la salle à manger et la cuisine, et offre un splendide panorama sur le golfe du Mexique. La spacieuse chambre à coucher et la bibliothèque se trouvent au dernier étage ; elles ont chacune une terrasse privative offrant un magnifique point de vue.

Ocean Boulevard

Urbanidad junto a la playa

La casa de tres pisos forma una sólida "pared" frente al patio de entrada sembrado de palmeras y se abre hacia el lado del mar a través de generosos frentes de vidrio. La planta baja contiene la entrada, piscinas llenas de reflejos, el garaje, el gimnasio y la piscina principal. Ésta fue ubicada en el lado sur de la casa, para aprovechar mejor el sol. Las áreas de estar, comedor y cocina se encuentran en el primer piso con vista al Golfo de México. El dormitorio principal y la biblioteca están en el piso superior, disponiendo de terrazas particulares y vistas panorámicas.

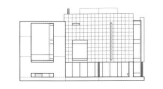

S

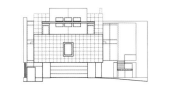

N

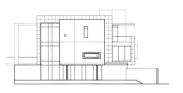

E

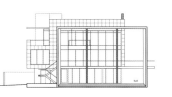

W

+1

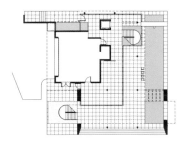

0

Terrace with a House

Hillside House in the Rain Forest

The steep hillside site inspired the architect to organize this home
on two levels. She foresaw the large living room with adjoining
kitchen on the upper level. A broad window ribbon spanned by
a reinforced concrete beam frames the breathtaking view of the
terrace and the Atlantic below. The bedrooms on the lower level
were deployed in front of the living room wing. Their roof forms
the generous terrace. Both terrace and living hall were paved with
small-format cobblestones, allowing interior and exterior spaces
to flow together and effectively merge house and nature.

Terrasse mit Haus

Hanghaus im Regenwald

Das stark abfallende Gelände inspirierte die Architektin dazu, die
Räume auf zwei Ebenen anzuordnen. Den großen Wohnraum mit
anschließender Küche hat sie auf der oberen Etage angeordnet.
Hier ermöglicht die Stahlbetonkonstruktion die Ausbildung einer
stützenfreien Öffnung zur Terrasse und zum atemberaubenden Ausblick
hin. Die Schlafräume der unteren Ebene lagern vor dem Wohnraumtrakt,
ihr Dach fungiert zugleich als Freiterrasse. Sowohl Terrasse als
auch Wohnsaal wurden mit Kleinsteinpflaster gepflastert, was die
wirkungsvolle Verschmelzung von Freiraum und Interieur verstärkt.

Une terrasse majestueuse

Maison à flanc de colline dans la forêt équatoriale

C'est le côté abrupt du site qui donna l'idée à l'architecte d'organiser la maison sur deux niveaux. Elle plaça donc la grande pièce à vivre et la cuisine attenante à l'étage supérieur. La construction en béton armé permit d'ouvrir une terrasse sans étai, qui offre une vue à couper le souffle. Les chambres à coucher de l'étage inférieur sont situées en avant de l'aile d'habitation ; leur toit constitue donc le fondement de la terrasse. La pièce à vivre et la terrasse ont toutes deux été pavées, mettant ainsi en valeur la fusion entre l'intérieur et l'extérieur.

Terraza con casa

Casa de ladera en el bosque tropical

El terreno fuertemente pendiente inspiró a la arquitecto a distribuir las habitaciones en dos plantas. La gran sala de estar con la cocina anexa se ubicaron en el piso superior. Aquí se ha formado una abertura no soportada hacia la terraza y con la impresionante vista. Los dormitorios ubicados en la planta inferior se anteponen al grupo de ambientes de estar y su techo al mismo tiempo sirve como terraza al aire libre. La terraza y la sala de estar se revistieron con piedras pequeñas, incrementando la efectiva fusión de espacio abierto y espacio interior.

Ubatuba, Brazil, Anne Marie Sumner, 1999, 450 m²

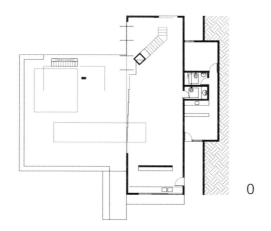

0

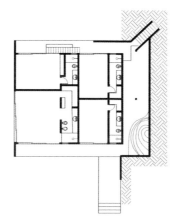

−1

Modern Tradition
Living on the Mediterranean
New houses designed on the Mediterranean Sea often employ forms of traditional Mediterranean architecture that can be traced back to Antiquity. This approach can easily result in banality as so many houses prove. At the same time, this method also offers the potential to reinterpret traditional forms to create a timeless modernity. Powerful, cube-like forms characterize the house complex with its white walls that stand in strong contrast to the earthen hues of the landscape. Nonetheless, the home seems in tune with the natural habitat that is dominated by the expansive view of the sea far below.

Moderne Tradition
Residieren über dem Mittelmeer
Bei Neubauten am Mittelmeer wird oft aus dem Formenkanon der traditionellen mediterranen Architektur, die bis zu den Phöniziern zurückverfolgt werden kann, geschöpft. Während solche Versuche häufig in Banalität enden beinhaltet dieser gestalterische Ansatz jedoch auch das Potential, das Traditionelle so auszuschöpfen, dass eine zeitlose Modernität entsteht. Kraftvolle, kubische Formen kennzeichnen den Hauskomplex, der mit seinen weißen Wänden im starken Kontrast zu den Erdtönen der Landschaft steht. Dennoch wirkt der Bau im Einklang mit der Umgebung, die vom weiten Blick auf das tief unten gelegene Meer geprägt wird.

Ibiza, Spain, Ramon Esteve Estudio de Arquitectura, 2003, 475 m^2

Modernité et tradition

Surplomber la Méditerranée

Les nouvelles constructions sur les sites autour de la grande bleue s'inspirent souvent de l'architecture traditionnelle méditerranéenne, qui remonte au temps des Phéniciens. Tandis que de tels projets s'avèrent le plus souvent banals, il demeure néanmoins possible d'appréhender cette approche créatrice en utilisant la tradition pour atteindre une véritable modernité intemporelle. De solides formes cubiques caractérisent cet ensemble, et ses façades blanches contrastent agréablement avec les tons couleur terre du paysage. La construction s'intègre cependant parfaitement à son environnement et offre un point de vue imprenable sur la mer Méditerranée.

Moderna Tradición

Vivir sobre el Mediterráneo

Las nuevas construcciones levantadas junto al Mediterráneo muchas veces se inspiran en el canon de formas de la arquitectura mediterránea tradicional, remontándose hasta los fenicios. Este enfoque también encierra el potencial de aprovechar lo tradicional de un modo que se crea una modernidad independiente del tiempo. Las vigorosas formas cúbicas caracterizan el complejo, cuyas paredes blancas contrastan fuertemente con los tonos térreos del paisaje. No obstante, la construcción parece armonizar con su entorno, caracterizado por la vista sobre el mar que yace abajo.

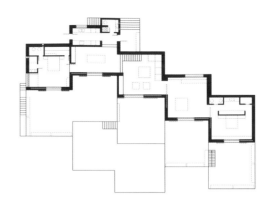

Bahia, Brazil,
Fabrizio Ceccarelli
2002, 550 m²

By Nature's Measures

A Pavilion in the Palm Forest

Reinterpretation of local traditions and response to climate formed the points of departure for this design – a comfortable residential oasis in the palms. The exposed structural framework constructed in planed tree trunks carries the roof of woven palm fronds. An informal sequence of interconnected spaces is defined under the protective roof with its wide eaves. The living spaces on the ground floor flow into each other and continue out to the exterior veranda and terraces. The floors were tiled with cooling, large-format ceramic plating. The warm hues of the floors are echoed by the glowing yellow and orange tones used on the walls.

Mit den Mitteln der Natur

Pavillon im Palmenwald

Die Weiterentwicklung lokaler Bautraditionen und Berücksichtigung klimatischer Bedingungen boten zwei Anhaltspunkte bei dem Entwurf dieser Wohnoase zum Wohlfühlen. Ein sichtbares Trageskelett aus behobelten Baumstämmen nimmt die dicht verflochtenen Palmenblätter des Daches auf. Unter dem Schutz des weit ausladenden Daches entwickelt sich eine Raumfolge diverser Wohnzonen, die im Erdgeschoss ineinander fließen und sich unter der Veranda und auf der Terrasse im Freien fortsetzen. Die Fußböden wurden mit kühlenden Keramikplatten und großformatigen Fliesen belegt, deren warme Farbtöne die leuchtenden Gelb- und Orangetönen der Wände ergänzen.

Utiliser les moyens naturels

Un pavillon dans la forêt de palmiers

La perpétuation des traditions locales de construction et la prise en compte des conditions climatiques ont influencé la conception de cette oasis de bien-être. Une charpente visible de troncs d'arbre dressés soutient les feuilles de palmiers finement tressées qui constituent le toit. Protégées par ce toit généreux, plusieurs pièces à vivre se succèdent au rez-de-chaussée pour se prolonger sous la véranda et la terrasse à ciel ouvert. Les sols ont été revêtus de plaques de céramique rafraîchissante et de grands carrelages, dont les couleurs chaudes s'harmonisent avec les tons éclatants jaune et orange des murs.

Con medios naturales

Pabellón en el palmar

Las tradiciones arquitectónicas locales y las condiciones climáticas fueron dos puntos de referencia en el diseño de este oasis habitacional. El esqueleto de troncos de árboles acepillados recibe el techo de hojas de palma. Bajo la protección del amplio techo se desarrolla una sucesión de espacios habitacionales que concurren en la planta baja y se prolongan bajo la veranda y en la terraza al aire libre. Los pisos se revistieron con placas de cerámica y grandes baldosas, cuyos tonos cálidos se complementan con los luminosos tonos amarillos y anaranjados de las paredes.

Guaecá Beach, São Sebastião, Brazil
Mario Biselli
2003, 693 m²

Room to Breathe

Hall House Typology

The site lies in the midst of the Serra do Mar coast range and the lush Mata Atlântica rain forest. The central living hall is the focus of the composition. It is enclosed on three sides and opens out via a glazed two-story window to a view of the nearby Atlantic Ocean. The upper floor houses four bedrooms and a TV room. Living and kitchen areas are located on the ground floor. The south and east perimeters are formed by terraces, verandas, and the elongated pool. Both on the interior and exterior, white surfaces are played off natural wooden surfaces to form an airy sense of generosity.

Platz zum Atmen

Hallenhaus Typologie

Das Grundstück liegt inmitten des Serra do Mar Küstengebirges und des Mata Atlântica Regenwaldes. Eine zentrale Wohnhalle bildet den Fokus der Komposition. Diese wird an drei Seiten räumlich gefasst und öffnet sich über eine zweigeschossige Glasfront zum Blick auf den nahen Atlantik. Das OG beherbergt vier Schlafzimmer und ein TV-Zimmer. Wohn- und Kochzonen befinden sich im EG. Nach Süden und Osten setzen Terrassen, Veranden und der lange Pool die Architektur im Freien fort. Sowohl innen als auch außen werden weiße Flächen gegen hölzerne Flächen gesetzt, um ein luftiges Ambiente der Großzügigkeit zu erzeugen

De l'espace pour respirer

Une maison aérée

Le terrain est situé au cœur du massif côtier Serra do Mar et de la forêt équatoriale Mata Atlântica. Une grande pièce à vivre constitue le centre de la structure. Comprenant trois murs pleins, elle s'ouvre sur l'Atlantique grâce à une baie vitrée sur deux niveaux. L'étage supérieur abrite quatre chambres à coucher et une salle de télévision. Le salon et la cuisine se trouvent au rez-de-chaussée. Au sud et à l'ouest, des terrasses, des vérandas et une grande piscine prolongent le style architectural à l'extérieur. Aussi bien dans la maison qu'au dehors, les murs blancs contrastent avec les surfaces couleur bois et créent une ambiance aérée et généreuse.

Espacio para respirar

Tipología de casa-hall

El terreno está situado en la sierra costeña Serra do Mar, en el bosque tropical de Mata Atlântica. El punto focal es un hall habitacional central. Engarzado por tres de sus lados, se abre a la vista sobre el Atlántico a través de un frente de vidrio de dos pisos. El piso superior alberga cuatro dormitorios y una sala de TV. Las áreas de estar y la cocina se ubican en la planta baja. Hacia el sur y el este, la arquitectura se prolonga al aire libre a través de terrazas, verandas y la piscina. Adentro y afuera se alternan las superficies blancas y las superficies de madera.

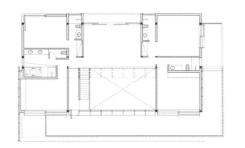

+1

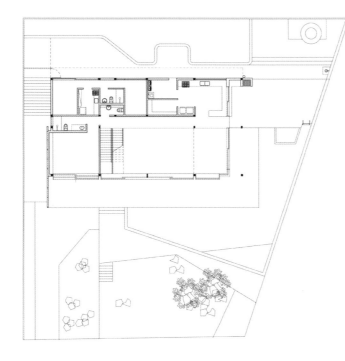

0

Colonnade on the Sea

Modern Temple Analogy

The guiding principle of this design was the creation of a temple-like concrete framework that forms a superstructure within which cube volumes containing the living functions were skillfully placed. The main living spaces for this four-person family are located in the elevated first level. The master bedroom suite, fitness spaces, a library, and guest quarters are organized on the second level and enjoy a roof garden. The cube volumes are interconnected by interior bridges and multi-level atrium spaces. The vibrant colors utilized were derived from the underside of a seashell found on the nearby beach.

Kolonnade am Meer

Moderne Tempelanalogie

Leitgedanke dieses Entwurfs war die Schaffung eines tempelähnlichen Betonrahmenwerkes. Die verschiedenen Funktionen des Hauses werden als farbenfrohe Kuben, deren Farben von einer in der Nähe gefundenen Muschel abgeleitet wurden, in dieses Rahmenwerk eingefügt. Der eigentliche Wohnbereich der vierköpfigen Familie befindet sich abgelöst vom Garten im 1. OG. Der Schlafbereich der Eltern, der Fitnessbereich, die Bibliothek und die Gästezimmer sind im 2. OG angeordnet und verfügen über eine begrünte Dachterrasse. Die Wohnkuben werden im Inneren über Brücken und mehrgeschossige Wohnhallen miteinander verbunden.

Des arcades en bord de mer

Un temple moderne

L'idée directrice de ce projet était de créer une construction en béton semblable à un temple. Les différentes pièces de la maison ont été intégrées dans ce cube coloré, dont les tons furent inspirés d'un coquillage trouvé à proximité du site. L'espace à vivre de cette famille de quatre personne se trouve au 1er étage, coupé ainsi du jardin. La chambre à coucher des parents, la salle de fitness, la bibliothèque et les chambres des invités se situent au 2ème étage ; elles disposent d'une terrasse ornée de verdure sur le toit.
A l'intérieur, les « cubes » d'habitation sont reliés entre eux par des petits ponts et plusieurs halls de communication.

Corredor de columnas junto al mar

Analogía moderna de un templo

El pensamiento central de este diseño fue la creación de una estructura de marco de hormigón similar a la de un templo. Las diversas funciones de la casa se integran en ella como cubos multicolores, cuyos colores se derivaron de una concha marina hallada cerca del sitio. La zona habitada por la familia de cuatro miembros se halla separada del nivel del jardín en el primer piso. El dormitorio de los padres, el gimnasio, la biblioteca y las habitaciones para huéspedes están en el segundo piso que incluye una terraza de techo sembrada con plantas. Estos cubos habitables se comunican en el interior a través de puentes y halls de varios pisos.

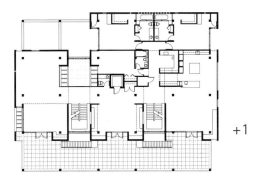

+1

Siesta Key, FL, USA, Guy Peterson / OFA Inc., 2000, 700 m²

Lagoa de Uruaú, Beberibe, Brazil
Gerson Castelo Branco
1999, 950 m²

Beach Bird

Thoughtful Integration of Building Mass

To avoid infringing on the exposed, lagoon natural setting with clumsy building masses the architect opted for embedding this three-story home in the natural slope. This allows it to integrate into the horizon as a seemingly one-story mass on the entrance side. But the steep, wing-like roof forms rise to contain an additional level with a complete bedroom wing. Another bedroom and a large living room with a roof terrace are located on the entrance level. The kitchen is located on the lower, beachside level. Here, covered exterior spaces with direct access to pool and beach serve as spaces for relaxation in the cooling shade under the house.

Strandvogel

Bauen mit der Topographie

Um die exponierte Lage an einer abgelegenen Lagune nicht durch störende Baumassen zu beeinträchtigen, wurde der dreigeschossige Bau in das Gelände eingepasst. Von der Eingangsseite wirkt das Haus eingeschossig, die steilen, flügelähnlichen Dachformen beherbergen jedoch auch ein komplettes Schlafgeschoss. Ein weiterer Schlafraum und ein großes Wohnzimmer mit anschließender Dachterrasse sind auf der Eingangsebene untergebracht. Die Küche befindet sich auf der unteren Ebene auf Strandniveau. Hier werden Raumbereiche im Freien in den kühlen Schatten unter dem Haus gebildet, die zum erholsamen Aufenthalt direkt am Pool und am Meer einladen.

Un oiseau sur la plage

Construire en respectant la topographie des lieux

Afin de ne pas nuire à ce paysage de lagune isolée, la construction sur trois étages a été spécialement conçue pour s'intégrer parfaitement à l'environnement. Lorsqu'on se trouve du côté de l'entrée, la maison semble être de plain pied ; le toit, pointu et semblable à des ailes, abrite cependant un vaste espace nuit. Une autre chambre à coucher ainsi qu'un grand salon avec terrasse surélevée attenante, ont été intégrés au niveau de l'entrée. La cuisine se trouve quant à elle à l'étage inférieur, qui donne sur la plage. A l'extérieur, astucieusement situés sous la maison, plusieurs coins d'ombre, offrant un accès direct à la piscine et à la mer, invitent à la détente et au repos.

Ave de playa

Construir en armonía con la topografía

Para no perjudicar su entorno expuesto a orillas de una laguna solitaria por la interferencia de las masas constructivas ajenas, el edificio de tres plantas fue adaptado al terreno. Desde el lado de la entrada, la casa aparenta ser de una sola planta, pero las empinadas formas del techo, semejantes a alas, incluyen también una planta entera con dormitorios. Otro dormitorio y una amplia sala de estar conectada con una terraza de techo se han ubicado en el nivel de la entrada. La cocina se encuentra en la planta inferior a nivel de la playa. Aquí, a la fresca sombra bajo la casa, se forman espacios y ambientes al aire libre que invitan a la recreación y el esparcimiento directamente junto a la piscina y el mar.

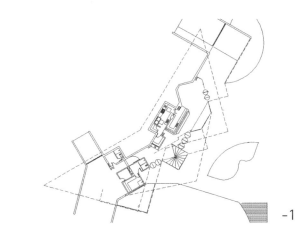
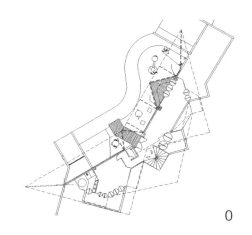

-1

0

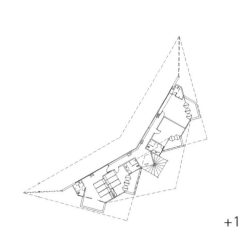

+1

Casa Poli, Coliumo, Chile
Pezo von Ellrichhausen, 2005, page 112

Pacific Houses

Am Pazifik | Sur la côte Pacifique | Junto al Pacífico

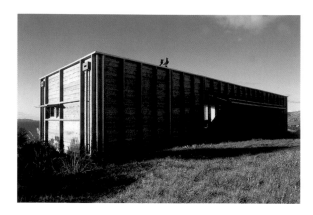

Coromandel Peninsula, New Zealand
Crosson Clarke Cornahan Architects
2001, 126 m²

A Container for Living
New Wood Construction Techniques

The house was conceived as a habitable container. Crafted in wood, it expresses structure, cladding, and joinery in a unique way. The unadorned natural timber creates a connection to nature. The decks can be hoisted to a closed position and become walls when the cabin is uninhabited. The simple rectangular building reminds one of a rural shed, facing north and the view. The living room is open to the outside and the sun, a metaphorical tent, while the bunkrooms are enclosed and cool. The fireplace allows winter occupation and the open bathroom and moveable bath allow the ritual of bathing to become an experience connected to nature.

Ein Container zum Wohnen
Neue Holzbauweisen

Das Haus wurde als ein bewohnbarer Container konzipiert. Die Primärkonstruktion, Schalung und Böden wurden komplett aus Holz erbaut, was eine eindrucksvolle Verbindung zur Natur schafft. Die Terrassen können hochgekippt werden, um geschlossene Wandflächen zu bilden. Das einfache Rechteck mit Nordorientierung zum Meer hin erinnert an eine Scheune. Das Wohnzimmer ist offen zur Landschaft und zur Sonne und bildet ein metaphorisches Zelt. Der offene Kamin ermöglicht auch eine Winternutzung. Das Bad kann zur Natur hin geöffnet werden, um ein Baden im Freien zu ermöglichen.

Vivre dans un container
Nouvelles méthodes de construction en bois

La maison a été conçue comme un container habitable. La construction primaire, la charpente et les planchers sont entièrement en bois, créant ainsi une parfaite harmonie avec la nature. Les terrasses peuvent être rabattues vers le haut et deviennent ainsi des murs pleins fermés. Ce rectangle aux mesures élémentaires, orienté vers le nord en direction de la mer, ressemble à une grange. Le salon s'ouvre sur le paysage côté soleil et constitue ainsi comme une tente imaginaire. La cheminée ouverte rend l'atmosphère agréable en hiver. La salle de bains peut s'ouvrir complètement permettant ainsi de prendre un bain à ciel ouvert.

Un contenedor para vivir
Nuevas técnicas de construcción en madera

La casa se concibió como contenedor habitable. La construcción primaria, el encofrado y los pisos se construyeron enteramente de madera, creando un vínculo con la naturaleza. Las terrazas se pueden levantar como puentes levadizos, para formar superficies de pared cerradas. El sencillo rectángulo orientado hacia el norte, hacia el mar, evoca el recuerdo de un granero. La sala de estar se abre al paisaje y al sol y constituye una carpa metafórica. La chimenea permite el uso durante el invierno. Incluso el baño se abre hacia la naturaleza.

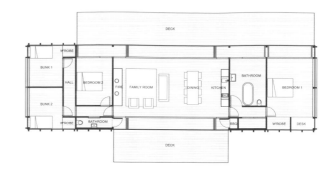

Little House in the Woods

Summer Cabin as Future Main Home

This summerhouse will become a retirement house for a couple and their extended family. The site slopes steeply down to the rocky beach and is forested with mature firs. The simple program was augmented by concerns that natural light be used in contrast to the dark forest. To do this, a thin continuous skylight at the roof peak catches the sun from early morning until late afternoon. Views east to the coast and mountains were maximized. In response to the owner's desire to be able to "use" the site, outdoor porches were added. A glazed roll-up garage door opens the workroom to the site. The porch and deck connect onto a trail leading down to the shore.

Refugium im Wald

Sommerhaus als späteres Haupthaus

Dieses Sommerhaus wird später zum Hauptwohnsitz eines Paares und deren Großfamilie. Das Grundstück fällt steil zum felsigen Strand ab und ist mit alten Tannen bewaldet. Das übersichtliche Volumen wurde durch Maßnahmen zum Einfangen des Sonnenlichtes im dunklen Wald gegliedert – ein Oberlicht in der Dachspitze führt ganztägig Licht ins Innere. Ausblicke nach Osten zur Küste und zu den Bergen werden betont. Auf Wunsch des Klienten wurden überdachte Veranden im Freien vorgesehen. Ein verglastes Rolltor erlaubt es, das Arbeitszimmer zum Wald hin zu öffnen. Von Verandadeck führt ein Waldpfad hinunter zum Meer.

Un refuge dans les bois

Maison de villégiature avant de devenir résidence principale

Cette résidence estivale deviendra plus tard l'habitation principale d'un couple et de leur grande famille. Boisé de hauts sapins, le terrain pentu descend jusqu'à la plage rocheuse. La maison a été réalisée afin de capter au maximum la clarté du soleil malgré l'obscurité de la forêt : pour cela, un bandeau a été ouvert dans le toit pour laisser entrer la lumière du matin au soir. Les points de vue côté Est, vers la côte et les montagnes, ont été mis en valeur. A la demande du client, des vérandas couvertes ont été ajoutées. Une porte roulante vitrée permet d'ouvrir le bureau sur l'extérieur. Depuis la terrasse de la véranda, un sentier boisé mène à la mer.

Refugio en el bosque

Casa de verano y futura casa principal

Esta casa de verano será la futura residencia principal de una familia. El terreno desciende a la playa y en él crecen antiguos abetos. El volumen abierto se estructuró con medios para captar la luz solar en la penumbra del bosque y conducirla al interior de la casa durante todo el día. Se realzaron las vistas hacia el este, hacia la costa y las montañas. A petición del cliente, se incluyeron verandas techadas al aire libre. Una puerta corrediza de vidrio permite abrir el cuarto de trabajo hacia el bosque. Un sendero desciende al mar.

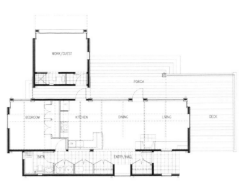

Guemes Island, WA, US, The Miller/Hull Partnership, 2001, 125 m²

San Juan Island, WA, US
Suyama Peterson Deguchi Architects
2001, 135 m²

Embedded in the Earth

Place-Making Design

The site is poised at the seam between two worlds, a typical suburban subdivision and the natural landscape above rocky headlands. This house and site are composed as a sequence of spaces that intensify the experience of the landscape and shield the visitor from the bland houses that border on the site. To respect site topography the house is embedded behind a new retaining wall that provides protection from the weather and screens the neighbouring houses. Floating above this wall a vaulted roof echoes the rolling topography. The materials – concrete, steel, and wood - reinforce the austere quality of this retreat.

Im Schutz der Erde

Ortbildendes Design

Das Grundstück liegt am Übergang zweier Welten, einer typischen Vorortsiedlung und der Urlandschaft hoch über der schroffen Felsküste. Haus und Grundstück wurden als Raumsequenz konzipiert, die das Erleben der Landschaft intensiv werden lässt. Um die natürliche Topografie zu berücksichtigen, wurde das Haus hinter einer neuen Stützmauer, die vor dem Wetter und dem Anblick der Nachbarhäuser schützt, eingebettet. Darüber schwebt das Tonnendach, dessen Form die rollende Topografie widerspiegelt. Die Materialien – Beton, Stahl und Holz – unterstreichen das erhabene Ambiente dieses Ort des Refugiums.

Protégée par le relief

Un design créé par le site

Le terrain se trouve au croisement de deux mondes : une petite agglomération et le paysage naturel surplombant la côte rocheuse abrupte. La maison et le site ont été traités comme un tout, afin d'intensifier l'impression ressentie à la vue de cet ensemble harmonieux. Afin de respecter la topographie du lieu, la maison a été enclavée derrière un mur de soutènement qui lui confère une protection contre les intempéries et un isolement par rapport aux maisons voisines. La maison est coiffée par un toit en forme de tonneau, qui semble flotter et s'harmonise avec le paysage tout en rondeurs. Les matériaux – béton, acier et bois – renforcent l'atmosphère particulière de ce hâvre de paix.

Protegida en la tierra

Un diseño configurador

El terreno se encuentra situado en la transición entre dos mundos, un típico poblado suburbano y el paisaje prehistórico a gran altura sobre la escapada costa rocosa. La casa y el terreno se consideraron como una secuencia espacial, que intensifica el hecho de experimentar el paisaje. Para tomar en cuenta la topografía natural, la casa fue colocada detrás de un nuevo muro de sostén que protege contra la intemperie y la vista de las casas vecinas. Encima se suspende el techo de tonel, cuya forma refleja la topografía rodante. Los materiales - hormigón, acero y madera - subrayan el magnífico ambiente de este lugar de retiro.

Decatur Island, WA, US
Suyama Peterson Deguchi Architects
2001, 140 m^2

More than a Summer House

A Composition with Three Volumes

Intended for use on weekends and holidays, the house is comprised of three separate structures joined by a concrete plinth and a large shed roof. The living space has large sliding glass doors that open on the southeast corner, allowing the landscape to extend in and the activities of living to extend out. Opposite the glazed wall of the living space a cluster of wood-sided volumes contain the remaining program - kitchen, bedroom and guest quarters. The careful placement of these volumes to one another and their relationship to the roof, plinth, and glass line provide a contrast to the open and expansive living space.

Mehr als ein Sommerhaus

Eine Komposition aus drei Volumen

Das Haus, das an Wochenenden und in den Ferien bewohnt wird, besteht aus drei getrennten Volumen, die über einen Betonsockel und ein Pultdach miteinander verbunden werden. Glasschiebetüren an der südöstlichen Ecke des Wohnraums erlauben eine großzügige Öffnung zur Landschaft hin. Gegenüber dieser verglasten Wand befinden sich mit Holz verschalten Baukörpern mit den restlichen Räumen – Küche, Schlafzimmer und Gästebereich. Die bewusste Platzierung dieser Volumen zueinander und zum Dach, dem Sockel und der Verglasung schaffen einen Kontrast zur großzügigen Offenheit des Wohnraums.

Plus qu'une résidence d'été

Une composition en trois volumes

Occupée pendant les week-ends et les vacances, la maison est composée de trois volumes séparés, reliés entre eux par un plancher en béton et un appentis. Des baies vitrées coulissantes à l'angle sud-est de la pièce à vivre offrent une large ouverture sur le paysage. En retrait de cet espace de verre se trouvent les différents éléments de la construction dont l'un possède un coffrage en bois. Ils abritent les autres pièces de le maison : cuisine, chambre à coucher et pièce pour les invités. L'aménagement astucieux de ces volumes les uns par rapport aux autres, leur relation avec le toit, le plancher et la baie vitrée, offrent un contraste intéressant par rapport à la dimension généreuse de la pièce principale.

Más que una casa de verano

Una composición de tres volúmenes

La casa, habitada durante los fines de semana y las vacaciones, está formada por tres volúmenes separados, conectados entre sí por un zócalo de hormigón y un techo de una sola agua. Las puertas corredizas de vidrio en la sala de estar se abren generosamente al paisaje. Frente a esta pared de vidrio hay otro cuerpo constructivo revestido de madera que contiene las restantes habitaciones: áreas de cocina, dormitorio y huéspedes. La distribución consciente de estos volúmenes entre sí y en relación al techo, el zócalo y las superficies de vidrio, forman un contraste con la generosa amplitud del espacio habitable.

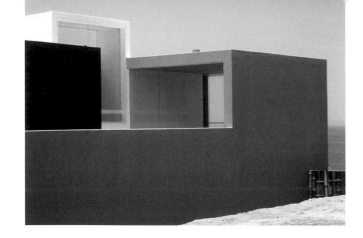

Poetry in Color

Hillside House on Coastal Slope

A creative design was conceived to integrate this home into the steep slope. An exterior stair leads down the side of the house from the entrance courtyard. The main entrance into the house is located on the first landing that gives access to the bedroom level. The living room was deployed on the lower, poolside level. It interconnects to the bedroom level above via a high, two-story spatial volume. Vibrant colors were employed to heighten the plasticity of the cube-like volumes that weather under the relentless sun of the Peruvian coast. The main house glows in a clear red tone, beige was used on the wall slabs that border to neighboring plots, and a white skylight tower creates a vertical focus.

Poesie in Farbe

Hanghaus an der Steilküste

Das Haus wird auf kreative Weise in die Hanglage eingepasst. Eine seitliche Treppe im Freien führt vom Eingangshof am Hang herunter. Auf dem ersten Zwischenpodest betritt man die Ebene der Schlafzimmer, ein Geschoss tiefer liegt der teilweise zweigeschossig ausgebildete Wohnraum auf der Poolebene. Leuchtende Farben werden eingesetzt, um die plastische Qualität der Baukörper unter der gleißenden Sonne der peruanischen Küste zu überhöhen. Das Haupthaus leuchtet in klarem Rot, beigefarbene Wandscheiben grenzen das Grundstück an beiden Längsseiten ab, und ein weißer Bügel wird als Lichtturm und vertikale Dominante betont.

De la poésie en couleurs

Maison surélevée sur la côte escarpée

La maison s'adapte de manière créative au paysage pentu. Un escalier latéral extérieur conduit de l'entrée au bas de la pente. Le premier étage intermédiaire permet d'accéder aux chambres à coucher ; un étage au-dessous, au même niveau que la piscine, se trouve la pièce à vivre, occupant en partie deux étages. Des couleurs éclatantes ont été utilisées afin de magnifier la qualité plastique des éléments de construction sous le soleil éblouissant de la côté péruvienne. Le bâtiment principal est rouge flamboyant, des parois murales beige longent le terrain sur les deux côtés de la maison et un arc blanc se dresse, apportant luminosité et verticalité à l'ensemble.

Poesía en colores

Casa de ladera

La casa se adapta de modo creativo a su ubicación. Una escalera lateral desciende desde el patio de entrada. El primer rellano intermedio lleva al piso de dormitorios. Un piso más abajo, al nivel de la piscina, está el área de estar parcialmente distribuida en dos plantas. Se usan colores brillantes para incrementar la calidad plástica de los cuerpos constructivos bajo el brillante sol en la costa peruana. La casa principal resplandece en rojo, paredes de color beige delimitan el terreno en ambos costados y un estribo blanco se realza como torre de luz y dominante vertical.

Cañete, Peru, Barclay & Crousse Architecture, 2001, 156 m²

0

−1

Cañete, Peru,
Barclay & Crousse Architecture,
2003, 174 m²

Carved Out Mass

Desert House on the Peruvian Coast

This house was conceived as a mass from which openings were "excavated", resulting in a merging of interior and exterior spaces. An entrance patio leads into the intimate space of the house towards the ocean and a large terrace with its long pool. The roof of the living/dining space hovers like a beach umbrella. Borders between the living/ dining space and the terrace are erased by frameless glass sliding panels. An open staircase follows the topography and leads to the bedroom level beneath the terrace. The children's bedrooms are accessed by a pergola covered by the terrace deck. The parents' bedroom under the pool is reached at the end of the staircase.

Ausgehöhlte Masse

Wüstenhaus an der Küste Perus

Dieses Haus wurde als eine solide Masse, aus der Stücke „gehauen" wurden, konzipiert. Der Eingangsvorhof führt Richtung Meer in das Hausinnere und zur großen Terrasse mit dem langen Pool. Das Dach des Wohn-Essbereichs schwebt darüber wie ein Strandschirm. Die Grenzen zwischen dem Wohn-Essbereich und der Terrasse werden dank der großen rahmenlosen Glasschiebeelemente fließend. Eine offene Freitreppe folgt der Topografie und führt Hang abwärts zur Schlafzone unter der Terrasse. Hier werden die Kinderzimmer über eine Pergola unter der Terrasse erschlossen. Das Elternzimmer unter dem Pool wird am Ende der Treppe erreicht.

Un bloc évidé

La maison du désert de la côte péruvienne

Cette maison a été conçue comme un bloc solide dont on aurait « taillé » des morceaux. En direction de la mer, un hall d'entrée s'ouvre sur l'intérieur de la maison, la terrasse et à la grande piscine. Le toit du salon-salle à manger flotte comme un parasol. Les limites entre la pièce à vivre et la terrasse sont quasiment invisibles, grâce à de larges baies vitrées coulissantes sans cadre. Un escalier extérieur ouvert, respectant la topographie, conduit aux chambres à coucher sous la terrasse. Les chambres des enfants sont accessibles par une pergola, et la chambre des parents, sous la piscine, se trouve au bout de l'escalier.

Masa excavada

Costa del Perú

Esta casa fue concebida como masa sólida, en la que se excavaron piezas. El antepatio de entrada conduce al interior de la casa y a la terraza con piscina. El techo se suspende sobre el área de estar / comedor. Los límites entre área de estar / comedor y terraza se confunden debido a los elementos corredizos de vidrio sin marco. Una escalinata abierta se adapta a la topografía y desciende a la zona de dormitorio bajo la terraza. Aquí se llega a las habitaciones de los niños pasando por una pérgola bajo la terraza. La habitación de los padres está al final de la escalera bajo la piscina.

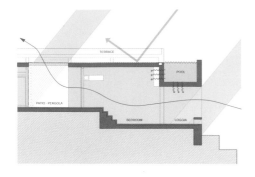

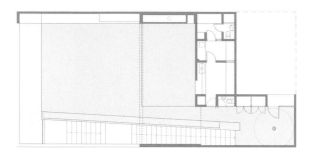

0

-1

High-Tech Home

Steel-frame House with Glass Facades

The rectangular plan is divided into three zones. The eastern zone is for the parents, the western zone for the children. The central zone contains the kitchen, living room, and dining area. An entry platform with an aluminum-louvered roof forms the entry to the house as well as a shaded veranda. On entering the house the dramatic view of the Pacific down the mountain to the south instantly opens up. Centralizing the living areas and pulling the service cores back from the glazing lines opens up striking diagonal vistas. To minimize the site impact of the building a lightweight steel structure was conceived.

High-Tech Haus

Stahlhaus mit verglasten Fassaden

Der rechteckige Grundriss wurde in drei Zonen unterteilt. Die östliche wird von den Eltern benutzt, die westliche von den Kindern. Die zentrale Zone umfasst Küche, Wohnzimmer und Essbereich. Eine Eingangsplattform mit einem Dach aus Aluminiumlamellen definiert den Eingang und fungiert zugleich als eine Veranda. Beim Betreten des Hauses öffnet sich ein freier Blick auf den Pazifik. Das Zusammenlegen der Wohnbereiche und Zurücksetzen der Servicekerne von der Fassade schafft reizvolle Diagonalblicke. Eine leichte Stahlkonstruktion wurde entwickelt, um das Grundstück möglichst wenig anzutasten.

Kiama, Australia, Engelen Moore, 2000, 160 m²

Maison high-tech

Architecture en acier et baies vitrées

Le plan rectangulaire a été divisé en trois zones. La partie Est est utilisée par les parents, la partie Ouest par les enfants. L'espace central comprend la cuisine, le salon et la salle à manger. Une plate-forme recouverte d'un toit en lamelles d'aluminium constitue l'entrée et sert également de véranda ombragée. En pénétrant dans la maison, une vue imprenable sur le Pacifique s'offre à vous. Le regroupement des espaces à vivre et la distance laissée libre par rapport à la façade créent d'intéressantes perspectives diagonales. Afin de nuire le moins possible au site, une construction spécifique en acier léger a été développée.

Casa de alta tecnología

Casa de acero con fachadas de vidrio

La planta rectangular se dividió en tres zonas. La zona este para los padres, la zona oeste para los niños. La zona central abarca la cocina, sala de estar y comedor. Una plataforma con techo de laminillas de aluminio define la entrada y sirve como veranda. Al entrar, una vista impresionante sobre el Pacífico se abre al observador. La agrupación de las áreas de estar y la relegación de los núcleos de servicio en relación a la fachada crea interesantes vistas diagonales. Se usó una construcción de acero liviana, a fin de tocar el terreno lo menos posible.

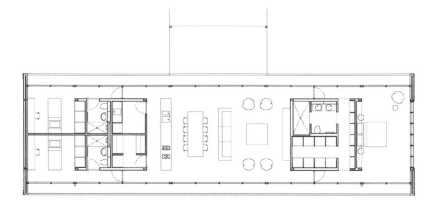

Coliumo, Chile
Pezo von Ellrichhausen
2005, 180 m^2

Solitude on the Cliff

House-Cube in Hand-Mixed Concrete

The remote, uninhabited location challenged the architects to respond with a unique architectural strategy. To express the remoteness and primitive quality of the site they created an especially raw ambience that reinterprets the stark clarity of the adjacent cliffs in built form. Inside, this rawness is countered by an intricately knit web of interior spaces. They extend up to skillfully connect the levels and define neutral hull for living, cultural, and exhibit use. Local workers used wood boards to build the concrete forms and poured the hand-mixed concrete layer by layer, largely without the use of conventional construction machinery.

Ruhepol an der Felsenküste

Würfel aus handgemischtem Beton

Der entlegene, fast unbewohnte Standort forderte das Architektenpaar zu einem ungewöhnlichen Ansatz heraus. Diesem ersten Bauwerk, das in diesem Landstrich je errichtet wurde, verliehen sie einen ausgeprägt rohen Charakter, der die Schroffheit der Felsklippen in Architektur fortsetzt. Dies wird im Inneren durch eine vielfältige Raumkomposition relativiert. Die Räume erstrecken sich teilweise über mehrere Ebenen und sind als neutrale Hüllen für Wohnen, aber auch für kulturelle Veranstaltungen und Ausstellungen, gedacht. Lokal engagierte Arbeiter verschalten den Bau lageweise mit handgemischtem Beton und vergossen ihn fast ohne Maschinen.

Un pôle de sérénité sur la côte rocheuse

Un cube de béton mélangé à la main

Le site isolé, presque inhabité, représentait un challenge inhabituel pour le couple d'architectes. Ils donnèrent à la première construction du secteur un caractère sobre, transposant ainsi l'aridité des falaises rocheuses au style architectural. La composition variée de l'aménagement intérieur vient compenser cet effet. Les pièces s'étendent en partie sur plusieurs étages et ont été conçues pour être des lieux habitables, ou pour servir à des manifestations culturelles ou des expositions. Les ouvriers locaux ont travaillé par couches successives et ont coulé le béton, presque sans l'aide de machine.

Refugio en la costa rocosa

Con hormigón mezclado a mano

El sitio alejado y casi deshabitado obligó a la pareja de arquitectos a buscar una solución poco usual. A esta construcción original le impartieron un carácter marcadamente tosco, integrando así la rudeza de los escollos marinos a la arquitectura. Esto cambia en el interior, donde las habitaciones se extienden por varios niveles, concibiéndose tanto como espacios para ser habitados, como también para albergar eventos culturales y exposiciones. El hormigón fue mezclado y vaciado a mano, prácticamente sin máquinas, por los obreros contratados localmente.

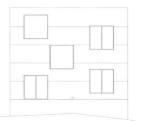

W

N

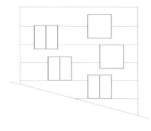

E

S

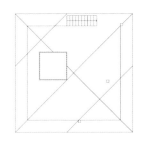

+3

+2

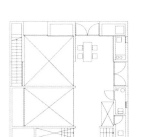

+1

0

At Wetland's Edge
Recovery of Natural Habitat

This site was formerly used as a burn pit by the local forest industry. This use resulted in major damage to the ecosystem. The architects therefore decided to place the house directly on the former burn pit and to re-naturalize the surrounding forest and beach landscape. First, the concrete foundations had to be excavated three meters deep into the former burn pit. Then the actual floor slab was constructed as an elevated platform upon which the living spaces were then erected. The L-shaped floor plan creates diverse views to the marina and the open sea. It also forms a wind-sheltered courtyard that is warmed by the morning sunlight.

Am Rande des Biotops
Neubau und Renaturierung

Lange Zeit wurden hier Baumreste, Abfall aus der Forstwirtschaft, verbrannt. Dieser Eingriff hat dem Ökosystem erheblichen Schaden zugefügt. So wurde entschieden, das Haus direkt auf der ehemaligen Verbrennungsstelle zu platzieren und die umliegende Landschaft zu renaturieren. Tiefe Fundamente wurden in die ehemalige Brandstelle gegraben, darauf entstand die leicht angehobene Fußbodenplattform mit den sich darauf befindlichen Wohnräumen. Der L-förmige Grundriss ermöglicht vielfältige Ausblicke zum Hafen und zum Meer hin und schafft zudem einen geschützten Außenbereich, der sich zur Morgensonne hin öffnet.

Proche du biotope
Le retour à la nature
Pendant de nombreuses années, des résidus d'arbres, issus de la sylviculture, furent brûlés sur ce terrain. Ce qui entraîna des dégâts considérables pour l'écosystème. Il fut donc décidé de construire la maison à l'endroit exact du foyer de combustion et de restaurer la nature environnante détruite. De profondes fondations furent creusées ; elles donnèrent ainsi naissance au plancher légèrement surélevé et aux différentes pièces de la maison. Le plan, en forme de L, offre de nombreuses vues sur le port et sur la mer, et a également permis de réaliser un espace extérieur protégé qui s'ouvre au soleil du matin.

Al borde del biótopo
Recuperación de la naturaleza
Durante mucho tiempo, aquí se quemaron restos de árboles y otros residuos forestales. Esta intervención causó severos daños en el ecosistema. Por ello se decidió emplazar la casa directamente sobre el antiguo sitio de quema y renaturalizar el paisaje circundante. En el antiguo sitio de incineración se excavaron profundos cimientos, sobre los cuales se construyó una plataforma ligeramente elevada con las habitaciones encima. El plano de planta en L ofrece múltiples vistas sobre el puerto y el mar, creando además un área exterior protegida.

Port Hadlock, WA, US, Eggleston Farkas Architects, 2002, 185 m²

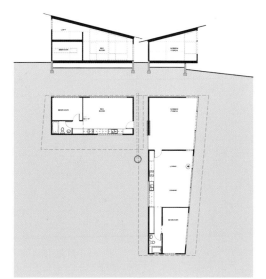

Stinson Beach, CA, US
Turnbull, Griffin & Haesloop
2004, 185 m²

Of the Dunes

Reinterpretation of a Classic House

This home was built to replace and commemorate a
beloved 1950's house by Willliam Wurster that was
severely damaged in a fire. Accommodation of new
earthquake and tsunami guidelines led the architects
to raise the structure on pier-like piles. These were
reinforced with exposed steel X-bracing as earthquake
protection. Flooding caused by a tsunami can flow
unimpeded under the house. The rooms are organized
in spatial ribbons. The living/dining space forms the
core of the composition. Diversely varied spaces with
direct connection to the dunes - a sheltered terrace
with an exterior fireplace, a broad stair with steps for
sitting, and a covered solar veranda - were foreseen.

Von den Dünen

Neuinterpretation eines Klassikers

Anstelle eines niedergebrannten William Wurster
Hauses aus den 50er Jahren wurde das neue Haus in
Anlehnung an das beliebte Original erbaut. Nunmehr
galt es, neuen Richtlinien zum Schutz gegen Erdbeben
und Tsunami zu entsprechen. Das Haus wurde
angehoben, um die Holzpfeiler des Fundaments mit
Stahlprofilen X-förmig zu verstärken und um eine freie
Unterspülung im Falle eines Tsunamis zu ermöglichen.
Die Zimmer sind in Raumbändern organisiert, der
Wohn-Essbereich bildet hierbei den Kern. Zum Meer
hin befinden sich Räume mit direktem Außenbezug:
eine geschützte Freiterrasse mit Kamin, Sitzstufen und
eine Sonnenveranda.

Au loin, l'horizon

La réinterpétation d'un grand classique

A l'endroit même où une maison William Wurster typique des années 50 avait brûlé, cette nouvelle maison a été construite, fidèle au prestigieux modèle original. Mais il s'agissait aujourd'hui de satisfaire aux nouvelles directives de protection sismique et anti-tsunami. La maison a été surélevée, des poutres de bois renforcées par des profils d'acier en forme de X ont été utilisées, permettant ainsi une libre circulation de l'eau sous la maison en cas de tsunami. Les pièces sont organisées autour d'un noyau central, formé par le salon-salle à manger. Les pièces ouvertes sur l'extérieur sont orientées vers la mer : une terrasse de plein air, abritée, avec une cheminée, des bancs creusés dans la pierre et une véranda ensoleillée.

La amplitud del horizonte

Reinterpretación de un clásico

Construida en el sitio antes ocupado por una casa William Wurster de los años 50, destruida por las llamas, la nueva casa se inspiró en el popular original. Cumpliendo con las nuevas normas de protección contra terremotos y tsunamis, la casa se elevó para reforzar los pilares de madera del fundamento con perfiles de acero en X y asegurar la circulación del agua en caso de tsunami. Las habitaciones están organizadas en bandas, donde el área de estar y de comedor forma el núcleo. Orientados hacia el mar hay ambientes comunicados directamente con el exterior: una terraza protegida al aire libre con chimenea, gradas para sentarse y una veranda de sol.

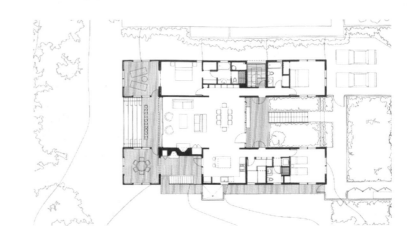

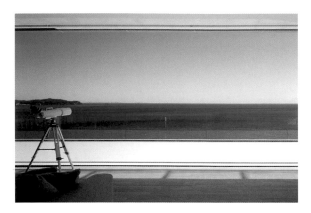

Atami, Japan,
Shinichi Ogawa
2005, 250 m²

Expansive Horizon
In Tune with the Natural
The site presented an opportunity seldom in Japan: the design of a residence with an unimpeded view of the sea. The architect responded to this challenge with uncompromising consequence. The salient line of the far horizon was directly translated into architecture. The living room and the large bathroom on the entrance level were foreseen with a dramatic ribbon window that creates a radical horizontality. Sliding glass window wall elements here allow the inhabitants to completely open the seaside facade. The bathing pool was set into the floor to heighten the sense of bathing in nature, a quality encountered in Japan's traditional "onsen" spas.

Dem Horizont verschrieben
Im Einklang mit dem Naturraum
Der Bauplatz bietet die in Japan seltene Gelegenheit, ein Haus mit ungehindertem Meerblick zu verwirklichen. Der Architekt antwortete auf diese Herausforderung mit einer kompromisslosen Konsequenz. Die ruhende Linie des weiten Horizonts wurde zum Hauptmotiv des Entwurfs. Die Wohnräume und das große Bad im Eingangsgeschoss des Hanghauses erhielten einen dramatischen Fensterband, der eine radikale Horizontalität erzeugt. Gläserne Schiebeelemente, die mittels Motoren geöffnet werden, erlauben die völlige Öffnung des Raums. In der in den Boden eingelassenen Wanne badet man, ähnlich wie in den traditionellen japanischen „onsen" Naturbädern, im Einklang mit der Natur.

L'horizon à perte de vue
En harmonie avec la nature
Le site de construction offre l'opportunité, rare au Japon, de réaliser une maison dont la vue s'ouvre complètement sur la mer. L'architecte en profita pour développer une œuvre unique. La ligne reposante de l'horizon lointain fut la base du projet. Les pièces à vivre et la vaste salle de bains, au niveau de l'entrée furent équipées de larges baies vitrées, créant ainsi une horizontalité infinie. Des éléments coulissants motorisés permettent une ouverture complète de la pièce. La baignoire, coulée dans le sol, offre la possibilité de prendre son bain en parfaite harmonie avec la nature, comme dans les bains naturels et traditionnels du Japon appelés « onsens ».

Entregado al horizonte
En armonía con el espacio natural
El sitio de construcción ofrece la posibilidad poco común en el Japón de construir una casa con vista libre sobre el mar. El arquitecto respondió a este reto con una consecuencia sin compromisos. La línea en reposo del lejano horizonte se convirtió en motivo central del diseño. Las habitaciones y la gran sala de baño en la planta de entrada a esta casa de ladera se dotaron con una dramática banda de ventanas que produce una horizontalidad radical. Los elementos corredizos de vidrio, accionados por motores, permiten la apertura completa del espacio. En la bañera empotrada en el suelo, el usuario se puede bañar en armonía con la naturaleza, similar a los baños naturales tradicionales japoneses.

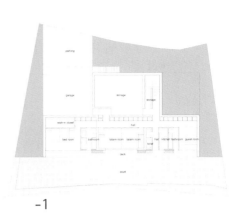

0   −1

At the Base of the Slope
Landslide-safe Construction

A former house here was destroyed when the adjacent slope turned into a mudslide. The new home to accommodate two families in separate wings was tailored to resist future slides. A robust plinth poured in concrete serves as the base for the main structural framework of wooden columns and glue-lam beams.

The goal was to capture the feeling of the regionally typical maritime architecture while at the same time providing protection from landslides. The only access to this home is via the foot path from the road above. The building materials, including the heavy concrete mixer trucks, were brought in across the sand bank at low tide.

Am Fuß des Hanges
Erdrutschsichere Bauweise

Ein Vorgängerbau wurde bei einem Erdrutsch zerstört. Um hier zwei Familien in getrennten Raumbereichen sicher unterzubringen wurde das neue Doppelhaus erdrutschsicher konzipiert. Ein stabiler Sockel aus Beton nimmt ein Tragwerk aus Holzpfeilern und Brettschichtholzbalken auf. Ziel war es, trotz dieser ernstzunehmenden Bedingungen die maritime Atmosphäre regional typischer Hafenbauten einzufangen. Ein Fußpfad von der hoher gelegenen Strasse aus bietet den einzigen Zugang. Baumaterialien, insbesondere die schweren Betontransporte, konnten nur bei Ebbe über den Strand angeliefert werden.

Au pied de la colline
Une construction anti-éboulement

Dans le passé, sur ce site, une construction fut détruite par un éboulement. Afin de pouvoir loger deux familles en toute sécurité, et dans deux espaces privatifs séparés, cette nouvelle maison double a été conçue pour parer aux éboulements. Un socle stable en béton soutient une structure portante de colonnes de bois et de poutrelles. L'objectif était, malgré ces conditions délicates, de reproduire le style maritime de la construction locale portuaire typique. Un chemin piéton qui mène à la rue située au-dessus de la maison, constitue l'unique accès. Les matériaux de construction, y compris le béton, ont donc dû être transportés à marée basse en passant par la plage.

Al pie de la pendiente
Construcción segura

Una construcción previa fue destruida por un deslizamiento de tierra. Para alojar aquí a dos familias de modo seguro, la casa doble se diseñó como construcción a prueba de deslizamientos. Un zócalo de hormigón recibe una estructura de pilares de madera y vigas de tablones. La intención fue captar la atmósfera marítima de las construcciones portuarias regionales. La única vía de acceso es un sendero que parte desde la carretera situada arriba. Los materiales de construcción, incluyendo el pesado hormigón, sólo pudieron acarrearse por la playa durante la marea baja.

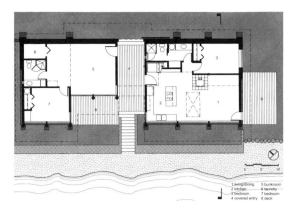

Normandy Park, WA, US, Balance Associates, 1998, 195 m²

Mornington Peninsula, Australia
SJB Architects
2003, 220 m²

View Platform with a House

Fully-Glazed Panorama Level

The typical lifeguard stations at local beaches served as a model for this house on Australia's Pacific coast near Melbourne. The elevated upper level built atop the flat roof platform formed by the ground level was foreseen with continuous aluminum-framed glazing elements. Wide eaves protect the glazed surfaces from the sun and also create shade for the expansive terrace that was surfaced with large-format ceramic plating. The main living spaces were foreseen with an open floor plan. The kitchen, dining, and living areas combine into a single space that seems large and generous in spite of its relatively small size.

Aussichtskanzel mit Haus

Vollverglaste Panoramaetage

Die typischen Kanzeln der lokalen Strandwachepavillons dienten als Vorbild für dieses Haus an der australischen Pazifikküste nahe der Millionenmetropole Melbourne. Das auf die Flachdachplattform des Erdgeschosses angehobene Obergeschoss wurde rundum mit Aluminium-/Glaselementen verglast. Ein weiter Dachüberstand schützt die Glasflächen vor der Sonne und spendet zudem Schatten für die große Terrasse, die mit großformatigen Keramikplatten ausgelegt wurde. Der Wohnbereich wurde offen gestaltet: Küche, Essplatz und Wohnecke bilden eine zusammenhängende Raumzone, die trotz der relativ kleinen Fläche großzügig wirkt.

Un belvédère en guise de maison

Un étage panoramique vitré

Les cabines typiques des surveillants de plage locaux ont servi de modèle à cette maison, située sur la côte Pacifique australienne, non loin de l'immense métropole de Melbourne. Tout autour de l'étage supérieur, qui repose sur le toit en terrasse du rez-de-chaussée, ont été posés des éléments d'aluminium et de verre. Une avancée de toit protège les surfaces vitrées du soleil et offre une ombre agréable sur la vaste terrasse, carrelée de grandes dalles de céramique. L'habitat a été conçu de manière ouverte : cuisine, salle à manger et pièce à vivre forment un espace communiquant et généreux malgré la petite taille de la surface allouée.

Mirador con casa

Piso con ventanales panorámicos

Los típicos puestos de vigía de los salvavidas de playa locales sirvieron de modelo para esta casa ubicada en la costa australiana del Pacífico, cerca de Melbourne. El piso superior, levantado sobre el techo de la planta baja, se encerró todo con ventanales de aluminio y vidrio. El amplio techo protege los ventanales contra el sol y da sombra a la gran terraza pavimentada con losas de cerámica. La cocina, el comedor y la sala de estar constituyen una zona de espacio coherente que a pesar del área relativamente pequeña produce una impresión de generosa amplitud.

+1

0

The New Beach Shack

Simplicity and Relaxed Living

Australians have long cherished the tradition of spending
the weekends and holidays in a simple beach shack. These
are characterized by lightness, cost-efficiency, and a strong
connectivity with the natural habitat. These qualities were creatively
reinterpreted here. Technical and support spaces were arrayed on the
ground level to form a base upon which the elevated living spaces
on the upper floor with their expansive view of the surrounding
landscape were placed. A mound was foreseen on the terrace side to
better embed the house into the landscape. This made it possible to
do without terrace railing and create an unimpeded view.

Strandhütte neu interpretiert

Einfachheit und entspanntes Wohnen

Schon seit langem pflegen die Australier die Sitte, die Ferien und
Wochenenden in einer einfachen Strandhütte zu verbringen.
Merkmale dieser Häuser sind Leichtigkeit, kostengünstige
Bauweise und den ausgeprägten Bezug zur Natur. Hier galt es,
diese Charakteristika neu zu interpretieren. Dienende Räume
wurden im EG angeordnet, um einen Sockel auszubilden, auf
dem sich die angehobenen Wohnbereiche im 1. OG mit Ausblick
in die Landschaft befinden. Durch Aufschüttung an die im 1. OG
gelegene Terrasse konnte auf ein Geländer verzichtet und ein
freier Ausblick in die Küstenlandschaft geschaffen werden.

Le cabanon de plage repensé
Un habitat tout en détente et en simplicité

Depuis longtemps déjà, les Australiens ont l'habitude de passer leurs vacances et leurs week-ends dans un cabanon de plage rudimentaire. Ces habitations se distinguent par leur style dépouillé, leur construction économique et leur harmonie avec la nature. Il s'agissait ici de réinterpréter ces caractéristiques. Les pièces de service ont été placées au rez-de-chaussée formant un plancher pour les espaces à vivre du 1er étage, qui offrent une vue sur le paysage. Grâce à un remblai rapporté sous la terrasse située au 1er étage, on a pu renoncer à construire une clôture, ce qui offre une perspective infinie sur le paysage côtier.

Cabaña de playa, nueva versión
Sencillez y vida relajada

Muchos australianos suelen pasar sus vacaciones y fines de semana en una sencilla cabaña de playa. Son características de estas casas su construcción liviana y económica, así como su proximidad a la naturaleza. Aquí se pretendió dar una nueva interpretación a estas características. Los ambientes de servicio se alojaron en la planta baja, formando un zócalo sobre el cual se ubican los ambientes de estar en el primer piso con vista al paisaje. Un terraplén que alcanza hasta la terraza en el primer piso permitió omitir una baranda y dejar la vista libre.

Flinders, Victoria, Australia, Jacksom Clements Burrows, 2002, 220 m²

Venice Beach, CA, USA
Lorcan O' Herlihy
2003, 230 m²

Vertically Stacked

Urban House on a Tight Lot

The tight urban parcel led the architect to vertically stack the required uses. An earthquake-proof steel frame structure allows the exterior wall surfaces made of glass and fiber-cement panels to be hung independently from the primary structural grid. The resultant architecture statement is thus defined more by the rhythm of the façade surfaces than by the box-like spatial volume of the house itself. This makes for the creation of especially unique, dynamic interior spaces. These were fitted out with furniture designed by the architect especially for this house. The view tower on the roof looks out toward the nearby Pacific Ocean.

Vertikal gestapelt

Stadthaus auf schmaler Parzelle

Die beengte städtische Lage veranlasste den Architekten, die Nutzungen vertikal zu stapeln. Die erdbebensichere Stahlrahmenkonstruktion ermöglicht es, die vorgehängten Fassadenelemente aus Glas und Faserzementplatten frei und unabhängig vom Konstruktionsraster zu verteilen. Es entsteht hierdurch eine Architektur, die sich mehr durch die Oberfläche als durch das räumliche Volumen definiert. Dennoch entstehen im Inneren spannungsvolle Räume, die durch vom Architekten eigens für dieses Haus entworfene Möbel komplettiert werden. Der Aussichtsturm auf dem Dach gibt den Blick auf den nahen Pazifik frei.

+2

+1

Tout en verticalité
Maison urbaine sur parcelle étroite

C'est l'étroitesse de ce site urbain qui incita l'architecte
à empiler les différents volumes de la maison. Une
construction antisismique, munie d'un cadre en acier,
leur permet de répartir les éléments de verre de la
façade et les plaques de ciment-fibre indépendamment
de la trame de construction. L'architecture résultante
se distingue ainsi par sa surface et non par son
volume. L'aménagement intérieur des espaces à vivre
est original ; le mobilier a été spécialement conçu
pour cette maison par l'architecte lui-même. La tour
panoramique sur le toit offre une perspective ouverte
sur le Pacifique tout proche.

Apilada verticalmente
Casa urbana sobre parcela estrecha

La restringida ubicación urbana motivó al arquitecto
a apilar verticalmente los espacios de utilidad. La
construcción con armazón de acero a prueba de
terremotos permite distribuir libremente los elementos
de fachada de vidrio y placas de cemento fibroso. Esto
resulta en una arquitectura que se define más por
la superficie que por el volumen espacial. Pero aun
así, en el interior se forman espacios emocionantes,
completados por el arquitecto con muebles diseñados
para esta casa. El mirador ubicado sobre el techo
ofrece una vista al cercano Pacífico.

Seola Beach, Burien, WA, USA
Eggleston Farkas Architects
2005, 226 m²

Beach Portico

Cube House with Bridge Access

This house was conceived to formulate an architectural transition between the steep adjacent hillside and the beach. A graceful steel bridge accesses the entrance and the two-level living room space beyond. This space creates a portal that forms a dramatic view through the house to the sea and celebrates the spatial transition between the city and nature. A private suite with sleeping areas is located on the upper level. The lower level, located directly on the beach, contains media, home office, and guest spaces. The wooden cladding with visibly exposed fasteners was purposely left untreated, allowing it to take on a silver-grey patina over the years.

Portal zum Meer

Wohnkubus mit Brücke

Zwischen einem steilen Uferhang und dem Strand gelegen entstand das Haus als Verbindung zwischen diesen landschaftlichen Gegebenheiten. Eine leichte Stahlbrücke führt zum Eingang und der zweigeschossigen Wohnhalle, die den Blick durch das Haus hindurch portalartig rahmt. Eine Privatsuite mit Schlafbereich befindet sich auf der obersten Etage, das direkt am Strand gelegene Sockelgeschoss nimmt Räume für Media-, Büro- und Gäste auf. Die Verkleidung aus Holzbrettern mit sichtbaren Befestigungen wurde unbehandelt belassen und wird im Laufe der Jahre eine silbergraue Patina annehmen.

Une porte qui donne sur la mer

Maison cubique avec ponton

Dressée entre une pente raide et la plage, cette maison semble être un intermédiaire entre les deux aspects du paysage. Un petit pont en acier conduit à l'entrée et à la pièce principale, qui met en valeur la vue de manière majestueuse. Une suite privée, avec chambre à coucher, se trouve à l'étage supérieur ; l'étage inférieur, au niveau de la plage, abrite la pièce multimédia, le bureau et un espace pour les invités. L'habillage en planches de bois, dont le scellement est apparent, a été laissé à l'état brut et prendra au fil du temps une patine gris argent.

Un portal hacia el mar

Cubo residencial con puente

Situada entre un acantilado y la playa, esta casa se formó como intermediaria entre las condiciones del paisaje. Un liviano puente de acero lleva a la entrada y el hall de dos plantas, enmarcando la impresionante vista a través de la casa. En el piso superior hay una suite privada con área de dormitorio, mientras que la planta baja, ubicada directamente junto a la playa, contiene ambientes de estar, oficina doméstica y atención de huéspedes. La madera del revestimiento no fue tratada, por lo que con el tiempo adoptará un color gris planteado.

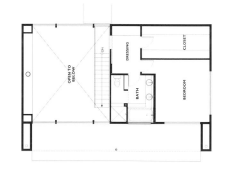

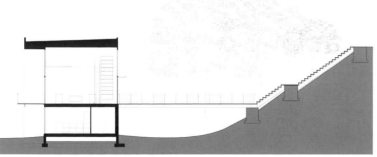

Malibu, CA, USA
Shubin + Donaldson Architects
2002, 260 m²

The Waves at Malibu

Light, Air, and Space in Spite of Density

The transitional entry courtyard introduces the primary design element of this home on Malibu's Pacific Coast Highway - the seamless union between interior and exterior spaces, with crisp linear architecture, ambulating plan, and visual access throughout. The ground-floor living room and adjacent sitting room offer serene respite from the sunlit terraces beyond, with cooling white and dark wood tones in the furniture and materials. The interior design palette of natural woods and limestone, white walls and fabrics, frosted and clear plate-glass creates a crisp and airy environment to appreciate the Pacific Ocean setting.

Die Wellen von Malibu

Licht, Luft und Raum trotz Dichte

Der Eingangsvorhof bildet einen wirksamen Übergang zu diesem Haus am Pacific Coast Highway in Malibu und verdeutlicht das zentrale Designprinzip – die scheinbare Einigkeit von Innen- und Außenräumen, linearer Architektur und Offenheit. Das im EG gelegene Wohnzimmer und der Salon daneben bilden Orte des Rückzugs von den besonnten Terrassen dahinter, was durch kühlende weiß- und dunkle Holztöne unterstrichen wird. Die im Inneren verwendeten Materialen - Kalksandstein, Naturholz, weiße Wände und Stoffe ergänzt durch matte- und klare Glasflächen - entsprechen der luftigen Leichtigkeit des direkt anschließenden Pazifiks.

Les vagues de Malibu

De la lumière, de l'air et de l'espace malgré la densité

La petite cour qui précède l'entrée de la maison symbolise le principe de design dominant de la Pacific Coast Highway à Malibu : la symbiose entre l'intérieur et l'extérieur, l'architecture en longueur et l'ouverture. La pièce à vivre et le salon, situés au rez-de-chaussée, permettent de se retirer de temps à autre de la terrasse ensoleillée, cette dernière offrant un élégant contraste par ses tons de bois blanc et coloré. Les matériaux utilisés à l'intérieur : le grès calcaire et le bois naturel, les murs et les tissus blancs, et les surfaces vitrées mattes et transparentes s'harmonisent avec la légèreté aérienne du Pacifique tout proche.

Las olas de Malibu

Luz, aire y espacio

El patio de entrada forma la transición a esta casa situada en el Pacific Coast Highway en Malibu y realza el principio de diseño central: la aparente unidad entre ambientes interiores y exteriores, arquitectura lineal y amplitud. La sala de estar en la planta baja y el salón adyacente, con sus tonos de madera blancos y oscuros, forman sitios para retirarse de las terrazas situadas más allá. Los materiales en el interior son piedra caliza, madera natural, paredes y telas blancas y superficies de vidrio opacas o claras que corresponden a la ventilada ligereza del Pacífico.

Sea of Tranquility
Minimalist Architecture and Design

The location on the Pacific Coast Highway led the architects to orient the house away from the road toward a protected entrance courtyard and the Pacific Ocean. In response to the direct exposure to weather and the elements on the beachside site the exterior shell of the residence was designed in robust exposed concrete. This minimalist vocabulary was also implemented inside, where the aesthetic reduction creates a pleasant ambience of healing. Inside, far removed from colorful, hectic Southern California outside, the light-filled, sheltered realm offers both visual and audible tranquility.

Meer der Stille

Minimalistische Architektur und Design

Die Lage am stark befahrenen Pacific Coast Highway ließ die Architekten das Haus konsequent zum abgeschirmten Eingangsvorhof und zum Meer hin ausrichten. Als Antwort auf die dem Wetter und den Elementen ausgesetzte direkte Meereslage entschied man sich, die Außenhülle des Hauses in robustem Sichtbeton zu erbauen. Dieses minimalistische Vokabular wird auch im Inneren angewendet, wo die Reduktion der Mittel ein wohltuendes, beruhigendes Ambiente erzeugt. Inmitten der bunten Hektik Südkaliforniens lebt man hier geborgen in einem behaglichen Reich der visuellen und hörbaren Ruhe.

Un océan de tranquillité

Architecture minimaliste et design

Le site, proche de la très fréquentée Pacific Coast Highway, a conduit les architectes à orienter la maison côté mer avec une cour d'entrée protégée. Pour répondre aux conditions climatiques et aux éléments naturels dus à la proximité de la mer, on décida de construire la structure extérieure de la maison en béton apparent. Ce style minimaliste fut également utilisé à l'intérieur, où le côté épuré du design crée une ambiance reposante et de bien-être. Au beau milieu de l'atmosphère animée et colorée du sud de la Californie, cette maison est un confortable paradis de tranquillité visuelle et auditive.

Mar de quietud

Arquitectura y diseño minimalista

La posición junto a la fuertemente transitada Pacific Coast Highway hizo que los arquitectos diseñaran la casa con un antepatio de entrada cerrado y orientada hacia el mar. En respuesta a la ubicación costera expuesta al tiempo y los elementos, se decidió construir el caparazón externo de robusto hormigón liso. Este vocabulario minimalista también se aplica en el interior, donde la reducción de los medios produce un ambiente tranquilizante y agradable. En medio de la colorida y agitada vida en el sur de California, aquí se vive en un mundo de tranquilidad para la vista y los oídos.

Ventura, CA, USA, DesignARC Architects, 2005, 280 m^2

0

+1

Bay of Islands, New Zealand
Pete Bossley Architects Ltd
1999, 330 m²

Architectural Camp

Articulated Rooms / Common Roof

The formative idea here was to reduce the elementary function of shelter to its essence and create a new notion of living on that basis. The indigenous architecture of the Pacific Islands – simple wooden pole structures with large roofs – was the direct precursor for this design. The linear floor plan descends along the hillside as it slopes down from north to south. The spaces, each of them designed as an individual room under the common roof, were interlinked to form a spatial chain. The prefabricated wooden structural framework and the roof were built first. Interior fitting and mounting of the window glazing were then easily executed under the weather protection provided by the broad roof.

Architektonischer Camp

Betonte Zimmer unter einem Dach

Grundprämisse war es hier, das Grundbedürfnis Obdach auf die elementarste Form zu abstrahieren und daraus eine neuartige Wohnwelt zu schaffen. Vorbilder der Bauform mit ihrem großen, auf Pfeilern lagernden Dach sind in der Volksarchitektur der pazifischen Inseln zu finden. Der lineare Grundriss folgt der von Norden nach Süden abfallenden Geländetopografie. Die Räume, jeder davon betont wie ein Einzelhaus unter dem großen Dach, wurden kettenartig angelegt. Zuerst wurden das konstruktive Gerüst und das Dach errichtet, danach erfolgte wettergeschützt der Innenausbau und das Stellen der Glaswände.

Un campement architectural

Des pièces de caractère sous un toit commun

L'idée de base du projet était de réduire la fonction d'abri à sa forme la plus élémentaire, et de créer ainsi un nouvelle définition de l'habitat. Avec son large toit, reposant sur des piliers, la construction s'inspire en grande partie de l'habitat populaire des îles du Pacifique. Le plan linéaire suit, du nord au sud, la topographie en pente du terrain. Les pièces, chacune semblant être une maison individuelle sous un toit commun, ont été disposées « à la chaîne ». Ce sont tout d'abord la charpente et le toit qui ont été construits, puis ont suivi l'aménagement intérieur et la pose des murs de verre.

Campamento arquitectónico

Habitaciones individualizadas

Aquí, la idea fundamental fue abstraer a su forma más elemental la necesidad básica de tener un techo y a partir de allí crear un nuevo mundo habitable. Ejemplos precursores se pueden encontrar en la arquitectura popular de las islas del Pacífico. La planta lineal sigue la topografía del terreno que desciende de norte a sur. Las habitaciones, cada una destacada como una vivienda individual bajo el gran techo común, fueron dispuestas en cadena. Primero se levantaron la estructura de soporte y el techo, después se realizó la construcción de los elementos interiores sin tener que exponerse a la intemperie, así como la construcción de las paredes de vidrio.

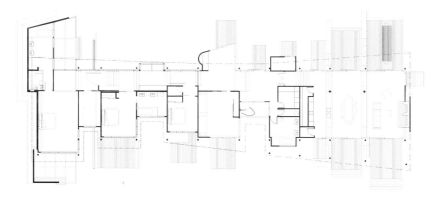

Newport Beach, CA, USA
Abramson Teiger Associates
2001, 390 m^2

Sailboat in Dry-Dock

Atrium Home with Rooftop Terrace

Sailboats from the nearby marina inspired the architects to translate the hovering lightness of their forms into architecture. This notion was pursued in the design of both the exterior volume and the interior central atrium space. The large roof terrace serves as a special exterior space for entertaining friends and business partners. The path through the house to the rooftop leads up the white steel stair in the central atrium. Bathed in natural light from the skylight, the atrium directs needed light inside where it is much needed due to the fact that external window openings were reduced by local planning constraints.

Segelboot an Land

Atriumhaus mit Dachterrasse

Segelboote vom nah gelegenen Marina inspirierten die Architekten, ihre schwebende Leichtigkeit in den Formen des Hauses nachzuempfinden.

Dieser Einfall wurde sowohl bei der Ausformung des Baukörpers als auch im zentralen Atrium konsequent umgesetzt. Die große Dachterrasse, auf der Besucher bewirtet werden, entspricht dem Wunsch der Bauherrschaft nach Repräsentationsflächen. Der Weg dahin führt über die weiße Stahltreppe im Atrium, das zudem die Funktion hat, Licht in die Tiefe des Hauses zu führen, denn Öffnungen nach außen wurden durch lokale planungsrechtliche Vorschriften begrenzt.

Un voilier à terre

Maison avec patio et terrasse sur le toit

Ce sont les voiliers de la marina voisine qui ont inspiré les architectes : leur élégance flottante a été transposée dans les formes de la maison. Ce concept a été appliqué non seulement à la forme extérieure de la construction mais également à l'aménagement du patio central. Le maître d'ouvrage souhaitait avoir une grande terrasse : construite sur le toit, elle peut accueillir de nombreux invités. On y accède par un escalier blanc, en acier, qui conduit tout d'abord au patio. Celui-ci a pour fonction d'amener de la lumière à l'intérieur de la maison. En effet, les ouvertures vers l'extérieur ont été réduites conformément aux prescriptions locales.

Un velero en tierra

Casa con patio y terraza

Los veleros de la marina cercana inspiraron a los arquitectos a imitar su flotante ligereza en las formas de la casa. Esta idea se realizó acertadamente tanto en el cuerpo de la casa como también en el patio central. En la amplia terraza de techo, usada como espacio representativo por los dueños, se atiende a los invitados y el camino hacia allí lleva por la blanca escalera de acero desde el patio. Este último tiene la función adicional de conducir luz a la profundidad de la casa, ya que el número de aberturas al exterior está restringido por las leyes locales.

Malibu, CA, USA
Kanner Architects
2003, 400 m²

Like Phoenix from the Ashes

Building on a High-Risk Site

This house, located in coastal hills that are periodically subject to bush blazes, was created like a phoenix rising from the ashes of a former house that burned down here. To reduce the risk of renewed catastrophe the new home was designed as a rectilinear volume and tiled with ceramic plating. This clear expression of its resistance to fire, poor weather, withering winds, floods, and earthquakes make it a powerful architectural statement that stands in marked contrast to the natural surroundings. Both interior and exterior spaces orient toward the west, the coastal hill landscape, and the sea beyond. The slim floor plan is especially conducive to natural ventilation.

Wie Phönix aus der Asche

Bauen in gefährdeter Lage

Gelegen auf Küstenhügeln, die periodisch von verheerenden Buschbränden heimgesucht werden, entstand der Bau wie Phönix aus der Asche eines niedergebrannten Vorgänger-Hauses. Um der Gefahr einer erneuten Katastrophe vorzubeugen, wurde ein schlichter, mit Keramikplatten verkleideter Baukörper entwickelt. Somit steht das Haus als Ausdruck seiner Widerstandfähigkeit gegen Brände, Wetter, Wind und Überflutungen bewusst im klaren Kontrast zur Umgebung. Die Räume sind nach Westen zum Meer und zur Hügellandschaft ausgerichtet. Der schlanke Grundriss erlaubt eine optimale Querlüftung durch die oft vorhandenen Meereswinde.

Comme un phénix qui renaît de ses cendres

Construire sur un terrain à risque

Située sur une colline côtière fréquemment soumise aux feux de forêt dévastateurs, la construction a été réalisée à l'endroit exact où une précédente maison avait brûlé : tel un phénix qui renaît de ses cendres. Afin d'éliminer le risque d'une nouvelle catastrophe, la construction a été revêtue de plaques de céramique. La maison est ainsi protégée du feu, des intempéries, du vent et des inondations, et contraste avec l'environnement. Les pièces sont orientécs vers l'ouest, en direction de la mer et du paysage de collines. Le plan, tout en longueur, permet une ventilation transversale optimale permise par les vents marins fréquents.

Como Fénix de las cenizas

Construir en sitio peligroso

Situada sobre colinas costeras periódicamente arrasadas por incendios forestales, esta construcción surgió como el ave Fénix de las cenizas de una casa anterior. Para prevenir una nueva catástrofe, se diseñó una sencilla construcción revestida con placas de cerámica. Así, la casa contrasta intencionalmente con su entorno, aludiendo a su resistencia contra los incendios, fenómenos meteorológicos e inundaciones. Las habitaciones están orientadas hacia el oeste, hacia el mar y el paisaje de colinas. La esbelta planta hace posible una óptima ventilación transversal por los abundantes vientos marinos.

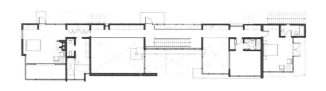

+1

0

Manhattan Beach, CA, USA
DesignARC
2000, 470 m²

The Zen of Building
Urban Hillside Home
The architects were faced with the difficult challenge of creating generous spaces for living on a small site with a directly adjacent neighboring house. In response, they integrated design elements found in traditional Asian residential architecture. Both the walled entrance courtyard with its tranquil fountain pond and the use of natural materials such as wood and natural stone document the creative reinterpretation of Asian precedents within a new context. Both here and there, the implementation of archaic architectural elements proves successful in creating harmonious spaces enlivened by light - even on the tightest sites.

Das Zen des Bauens
Urbanes Hanghaus
Das Architektenteam sah sich mit einer komplexen Aufgabe konfrontiert: die Schaffung eines großzügigen Ambientes auf der relativ kleinen Parzelle. Als Antwort hierauf wurde auf Elemente der asiatischen Wohnarchitektur zurückgegriffen. Der von Wänden umschlossene Eingangshof mit begehbarem Brunnenteich und der Einsatz von Naturmaterialien wie Holz und Naturstein zeugen von dieser produktiven Auseinandersetzung mit der Wohnarchitektur Asiens. Hier wie dort erweist sich dieser Einsatz von archaischen Architekturelementen als erfolgreich darin, eine von Licht belebte Harmonie auf engem Raum zu erzeugen.

Une construction zen

Une maison urbaine à flanc de colline

L'équipe d'architectes s'est vue confrontée à un exercice difficile : la création d'un espace généreux sur une parcelle relativement petite. Pour y répondre, ils firent appel à plusieurs principes de l'architecture de l'habitat asiatique. La cour d'entrée, entourée d'un mur, et son bassin, orné d'une fontaine, ainsi que l'utilisation de matériaux naturels comme le bois et la pierre sont les témoins d'une transposition réussie de l'architecture asiatique. Çà et là, l'utilisation d'éléments architecturaux archaïques se révèle subtile, tant la lumière qui pénètre dans la bâtisse crée une ambiance harmonieuse malgré une place réduite.

El Zen de la construcción

Casa de montaña urbana

Los arquitectos se enfrentaron a una tarea compleja: la creación de un ambiente generoso sobre una parcela relativamente pequeña. Se decidió recurrir a los elementos de la arquitectura residencial asiática. Un patio de entrada cerrado que incluye un estanque transitable, así como el empleo de materiales naturales como madera y piedra natural, son testimonios de esta confrontación con la arquitectura residencial del Asia. Aquí como allá, el uso de elementos arquitectónicos arcaicos sirve para crear una armonía vitalizada por la luz en espacios reducidos.

Semiahmoo, WA, USA
Nils Finne Associates
2001, 620 m²

Of Stone and Wood

Wood-Crafted House on Granite Plinth

The evocative qualities of wood and stone were explored here to effectively embed the home into the larger order of nature. The plinth of the hillside residence was clad in Canadian granite to create a massive base. The structural framework that rises above it was constructed in wood columns and roof beams and clad with wood shingles. Wood surfaces are also the formative element inside the interior spaces where they are combined with white wall surfaces to create a light, open ambience. This sense of light-filled airiness is strengthened by the roofs as they rise toward clerestory glazing on the building edges and bathe the interiors in natural light.

Von Stein und Holz

Holzhaus auf Sockel aus Granit

Die evokativen Kräfte von Holz und Stein werden hier mit dem Ziel zusammengeführt, das Haus in die größere Ordnung der Natur harmonisch einzubetten. So wurde das Sockelgeschoss des am Hang gelegenen Baus aus kanadischem Granit erbaut. Darüber baute man die tragenden Stützen und Dachträger aus Holz auf, die Wandflächen wurden dann mit Holzschindeln verschalt. Auch im Inneren ist Holz das prägende Material. Hier wird es mit weißen Wandflächen kombiniert, um eine helle, offene Qualität zu erzeugen. Dies wird durch den großzügigen Lichteinfall, den die nach außen ansteigenden Dächer bewirken, zusätzlich verstärkt.

De pierre et de bois

Une maison de bois sur un socle de granit

Le bois et la pierre ont été choisis pour leur aspect brut, et réunis dans le but de créer une maison s'intégrant parfaitement à la nature environnante. Ainsi, le fondement de cette maison à flanc de colline a été réalisé en granit canadien. Par-dessus, les poutres porteuses et les piliers du toit ont été exécutés en bois ; les surfaces murales, quant à elles, ont été revêtues d'un bardage de bois. A l'intérieur également, le bois est le matériel dominant. Combiné aux surfaces murales blanches, il crée une atmosphère lumineuse et ouverte. Cette clarté est encore renforcée par les larges ouvertures qu'offrent les toits obliques.

De piedra y madera

Casa de madera sobre granito

Las fuerzas evocadoras de la madera y la piedra se reúnen aquí con el objeto de integrar la casa armónicamente al orden superior de la naturaleza. Así, la planta del zócalo se construyó de granito canadiense. Encima se colocaron las estructuras de soporte y las vigas del techo de madera, mientras que las superficies de las paredes fueron revestidas con ripias de madera. En el interior también predomina la madera. Aquí se combina con paredes blancas, para producir la impresión de claridad y amplitud. Los techos ascendentes hacia afuera refuerzan esta impresión.

A Treasure in Wood

House Group at the Forest's Edge

In 2000, when the media reported the surfacing of huge wooden members that had dislodged after lying submerged for 80 years in a shipwreck sunk in 1921, the owners travelled there and procured several of the finest members. The house design integrated these historic finds as massive columns and beams that form an imposingly evocative structure reminiscent of grand mountain lodges. Two fireplace chimneys clad in natural stone nest within this wooden superstructure and form the focal points of the inside. The roof beams extend out to the exterior where they define the sheltered entrance zone and covered terraces.

Indian Ocean Houses

Am Indischen Ozean ⏐ A proximité de l'Océan Indien ⏐ Junto al Océano Índico

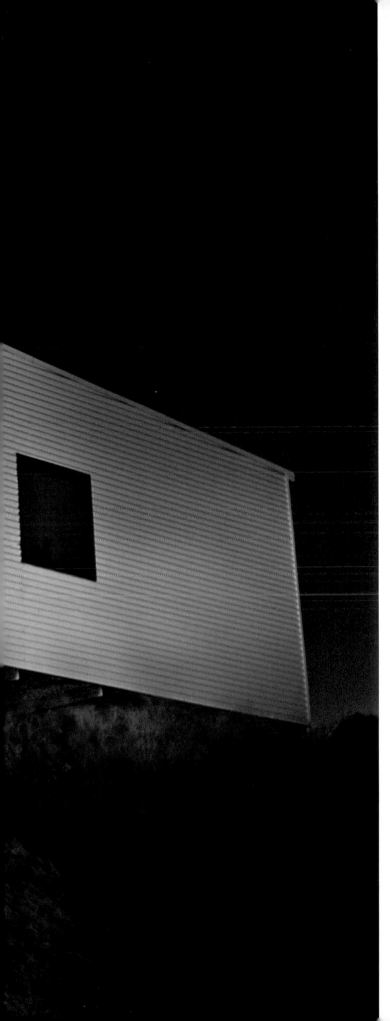

Dawesville, Australia
Iredale Pedersen Hook,
2002, 200 m²

Hovering Habitat

Stilt House in the Dunes

On his first visit to the site the architect discovered a local, 1950's house typology. These homes were raised above ground to provide protection from insects and dampness, and to maximize cooling winds in the hot climate. On this impulse it was decided to consequently raise the new home above plenum. The dramatic red wedge house seemingly hovers, supported merely by thin steel stilts. The hillside site additionally creates a protected space underneath the house that is used as an exterior living room during the region's long warm season. The innovative home was successfully built within the tight financial budget available.

Ein schwebendes Habitat

Stelzenhaus in Dünenlandschaft

Bei seinem Erstbesuch vor Ort entdeckte der Architekt einen hier häufigen Haustyp aus den 50er Jahren. Diese Häuser wurden vom Terrain gelöst, um sie vor Feuchtigkeit, Insekten und Tieren zu schützen und eine kühlende Luftumspülung in dem heißen Klima zu erreichen. Angeregt hiervon wurde entschieden, das neue Haus ebenfalls vom Plenum zu lösen. Hier erfolgt dies auf dramatische Weise: leichte Stahlstelzen lassen die Masse des Hauses schweben. Die Hanglage lässt unter dem Haus ein überdachtes Wohnzimmer im Freien entstehen. Das Haus wurde innerhalb eines engen Finanzrahmens erfolgreich realisiert.

Un habitat flottant

Maison surélevée dans les dunes

Lors de sa première visite sur le site, l'architecte y découvrit un type de maison courant dans les années 50. Ces maisons étaient rehaussées du terrain, afin de les protéger de l'humidité, des insectes et des animaux et également dans le but de lutter contre le climat très chaud par une ventilation rafraîchissante. Suivant cette idée, on décida de séparer aussi la nouvelle maison de sa base. Ce qui donne à la construction un profil vraiment hors du commun : de fines échasses en acier donnent l'impression que la maison flotte. Sous la maison se trouve ainsi un salon de plein air, couvert. La maison a été réalisée en respectant un budget limité.

Hábitat suspendido

Una casa sobre zancos entre las dunas

En su primera visita al sitio, el arquitecto descubrió un tipo de casa originado en los años 50 que aquí se veía con frecuencia. Estas casas se desprendían del terreno, a fin de protegerlas contra la humedad, los insectos y los animales y para producir una circulación de aire refrescante en este clima caliente. Motivado por esto, se decidió que la nueva casa también se desprendería del pleno. Esto se realizó de un modo dramático: La masa de la casa quedó suspendida sobre ligeros zancos de acero. La ubicación en la pendiente dio origen a la creación de una sala de estar techada al aire libre debajo de la casa. La casa fue realizada con éxito dentro de un estrecho marco financiero.

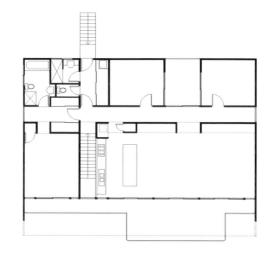

+1

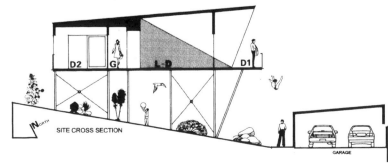

SITE CROSS SECTION

GARAGE

Adelaide, Australia
Con Bastiras Architect
2002, 500 m²

Perforated Cubes

Courtyard House Typology

The public beach promenade in Gleneig, a suburb of Adelaide, fronts directly onto the site. This led the architect to orient the home both toward the sea and to an inner courtyard with pool. A U-shaped floor plan encloses the private courtyard to the north of the house. The living spaces underscore this principle: the open living/dining realm with orientation to the beach is complemented by a second, more informal living room with a view of the private courtyard. The choice of cool, neutral materials creates a sense of pleasant understatement within which the delicate mix of informal and formal living functions are skillfully integrated.

Perforierte Kuben

Hofhaus Typologie

Die öffentliche Uferpromenade des Adelaide-Vororts Gleneig schließt direkt an das Grundstück an. So entschied der Architekt, das Haus zum Meer und zu einem privaten Wohnhof mit Pool auszurichten. Hierzu wurde ein U-förmiger Grundriss entwickelt, der einen im Norden des Hauses uneinsehbaren Hof bildet. Diesem Prinzip folgend wurden die Wohnbereiche angeordnet: zusätzlich zum offenen Wohn-Essbereich mit Meeresblick wurde ein informelles Wohnzimmer mit Hofausrichtung vorgesehen. Die zurückhaltende Materialienpalette bildet einen neutralen Rahmen für den Mix aus informellen und repräsentativen Wohnfunktionen.

Des cubes perforés

Un concept de maison avec cour

La promenade publique le long de la baie, au village Gleneig, voisin d'Adélaïde, passe le long du terrain de cette maison. C'est pourquoi l'architecte décida d'orienter l'habitation vers la mer et de construire une cour privative avec piscine. Pour cela, un plan en forme de U a été développé, créant une cour isolée du côté nord de la maison. Les différentes pièces ont été ensuite ordonnées en tenant compte de cette particularité : en complément de l'espace à vivre et de la cuisine ouverte, un salon informel donnant sur la cour a été aménagé. La palette sobre des matériaux offre un cadre neutre à ce mélange de fonctionnalités informelles et classiques.

Cubos perforados

Tipología de casa con patio

El paseo costeño público en Gleneig, suburbio de Adelaide, se conecta directamente con el terreno. Por esta razón, el arquitecto decidió orientar la casa hacia el mar y hacia un patio con piscina. Se diseñó una planta U que forma un patio no visible desde afuera en el lado norte de la casa. Las áreas de estar se distribuyeron siguiendo este principio: además de un área abierta de sala de estar y comedor con vista al mar, se incluyó una sala de estar informal orientada hacia el patio. La modesta gama de materiales empleados constituye un marco neutral para esta mezcla de funciones habitacionales informales y representativas.

Seabird Refuge

Wood Home with Organic Forms

This house, designed to accommodate four related families, is sited to maximize the full potential of solar gain and heighten protection against prevailing winds. It opens to the north where grassed terraces, a swimming pool and sundeck are protected from the south-western winds. All rooms have views of the surrounding coastlines. Conceptually, the house is both a refuge and a built metaphor of a seabird. Like a seagull bobbing on a giant swell it offers refuge from the blustering and capricious Bass Strait weather and its forms remind of birds that soar above the adjacent sea bluffs.

Meeresvogel Refugium

Holzhaus mit organischen Formen

Dieses Haus, das vier Familien als Wochenend- und Feriendomizil dient, wurde unter Einbeziehung der Sonne und Berücksichtigung der starken Windböen entworfen. Es öffnet sich nach Norden zu mit Dünengras bepflanzten Terrassen, zum Pool und zum Sonnendeck, die alle durch die Baukörper von harschen Windböen aus dem Südwesten geschützt werden. Die Formen des Haus-Refugiums lehnen sich metaphorisch an Meeresvögel an. Wie eine Möwe auf der Spitze einer sanften Welle bietet es Schutz gegen windiges und kapriziöses Wetter und erinnert an die Vögel, die über die nah gelegenen Klippen in die Höhe steigen.

Un refuge pour les oiseaux marins

Maison en bois et formes naturelles

Cette maison, qui peut servir de résidence secondaire ou de maison de vacances pour quatre familles, a été développée en tenant compte du soleil et des fortes rafales de vent. Elle est ouverte côté nord avec des terrasses plantées de végétation typique des dunes, une piscine et un solarium, le tout étant ainsi protégé du vent du sud-ouest grâce aux différentes parties de la construction. Les formes de cette maison-refuge rappellent celles des oiseaux marins. Comme une mouette sur le sommet d'une douce vague, elle offre un refuge contre le temps venté et capricieux. Elle fait penser aussi aux oiseaux qui se réfugient sur les hauteurs des falaises avoisinantes.

Refugio de ave marina

Casa de madera con formas orgánicas

Este domicilio de vacaciones y fines de semana para cuatro familias se diseñó considerando la incidencia del sol y los fuertes vientos. Se abre al norte con terrazas sembradas, en dirección a la piscina y la terraza de sol, protegidas por los edificios contra el viento del sudoeste. Las formas de este refugio-casa se inspiran metafóricamente en las aves marinas. Como una gaviota sobre la cresta de una ola, la casa ofrece refugio contra la intemperie, evocando el recuerdo de los pájaros que se remontan a las alturas sobre los cercanos escollos.

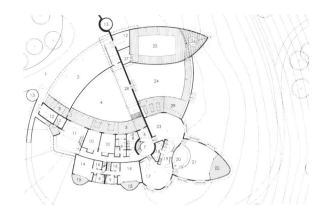

Flinders, Australia, Gregory Burgess Architects, 2000, 600 m²

Lake House, Berlin, Germany
Naegeli Architekten, 2002, page 140

Lakeside Houses

Wohnen am See | Vivre au bord d'un lac | Vivir junto al lago

Berlin, Germany,
Nägeli Architekten,
2002, 96 m²

New Memories

Lakeside House

An old, memory-imbued, 1930's summer house on the site was replaced with a new home that effectively transcends the ever present associations of the old. Room sizes and distribution of uses echo those of the razed predecessor. The wood-frame house was erected along the existing foundation line. The wood structure extends to form a pergola that integrates the house with its lakeside surroundings. Red cedar was used for wood sheathing on the exterior. White-stained maple, leather and lacquered surfaces were used to create a maritime atmosphere inside.

Neue Erinnerungen

Haus am See

Ein mit Erinnerungen behaftetes Sommerhaus aus den 1930er Jahren wird durch ein neues Haus ersetzt, das eingeprägte Assoziationen transzendiert. Die Dimensionen und die Disposition der Räume des abgebrochenen Hauses wurden weitgehend erhalten. Das Holzhaus folgt sorgfältig den vorhandenen Fundamenten. Die Holzkonstruktion setzt sich im Freien in einer Pergola fort, die das Haus mit der umliegenden Seenlandschaft verbindet. Die Außenhülle besteht aus Zedernholz, die Oberflächen im Innern aus weiß lasiertem Ahorn, Leder und farbig lackierten Oberflächen.

Un souvenir tout neuf

Maison en bord de lac

Une ancienne maison des années 1930, noyée dans la mémoire, a été remplacée sur ce terrain par une nouvelle habitation qui transcende en fait des souvenirs toujours présents. La taille et la distribution des pièces reproduisent celles de la maison rasée. Cette maison à structure en bois a été bâtie sur les anciennes fondations. Cette structure se prolonge par une pergola qui assure la transition avec l'environnement lacustre. Le revêtement extérieur est en cèdre rouge. Le bois d'érable cérusé, le cuir et les surfaces laquées concourent à la création d'une ambiance marine à l'intérieur.

Nuevas memorias

Casa del Lago

Una vieja casa de verano llena de recuerdos y construida en la década de 1930 ha sido sustituida por una nueva que transciende las siempre presentes asociaciones con la antigua construcción. Se mantuvieron las dimensiones y la disposición de los espacios de la vieja casa. La estructura de madera respeta los fundamentos ya existentes y se extiende además hasta una pérgola que une la casa con el paisaje del cercano lago. En el exterior se empleó madera roja de cedro, mientras que en el interior se utilizaron la madera de arce con veladura blanca, el cuero y las superficies de diferentes colores para recrear una atmósfera marina.

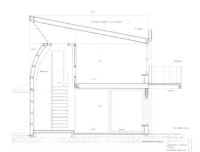

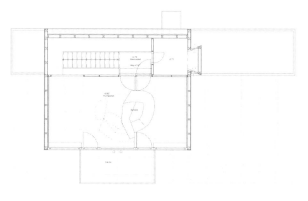

+1

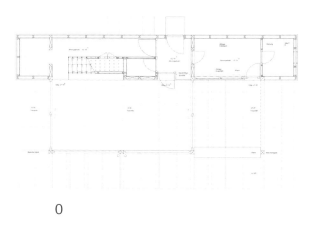

0

Northern Idaho, USA
Olson Sundberg Kundig Allen
2003, 316 m²

Door to the Wilderness

Wood Home with Organic Forms

This home, conceived as a simple shelter in nature, celebrates the untouched wilderness on the other side of the lake. A large glazed window element can be pivoted upward to create an opening across the entire width of the living room space that frames a portal view of the mountain silhouette. Following the example set by the simple cabins nearby, industrially fabricated materials were utilized: concrete block masonry was used for the walls, the living room floor is made of exposed concrete, basic steel profiles were used for window frames and roof beams, and a segment of steel pipe was transformed into an open fireplace.

Portal zur Wildnis

Holzhaus mit organischen Formen

Dieses Haus, als einfache Hütte in der Natur gedacht, zelebriert die unberührte Wildnis auf der anderen Seite des Sees. Ein großes Glasportal, das sich nach oben drehen lässt, schafft eine Öffnung über die ganze Breite des Wohnsaals, dessen Portalöffnung den Blick auf die Bergsilhouette rahmt. Dem Vorbild einfacher Behausungen der Gegend folgend wurden industriell gefertigte Materialien verwendet: die Wände sind aus Betonsteinen gemauert, der Boden des Wohnsaals ist aus Sichtbeton, einfache Stahlprofile wurden als Fensterrahmen und Deckenträger eingebaut und ein Stahlrohrsegment wurde in einen offenen Kamin umgewandelt.

Une porte ouverte sur la nature sauvage

Maison de bois aux formes naturelles

Cette maison a été conçue comme une simple cabane dans la nature et rend hommage au paysage immaculé situé sur la rive opposée du lac. Un imposant portail vitré, d'une largeur égale à celle de la pièce à vivre, s'ouvre en coulissant vers le haut et, vu de l'intérieur, son encadrement nous suggère un magnifique tableau de paysage montagneux. Suivant l'exemple des maisons classiques de la région, des matériaux industriels ont été utilisés pour la construction : les murs sont en béton, le plancher de la pièce à vivre est en béton apparent, des profilés en acier servent de cadres de fenêtres et de poutres, et un segment de tube d'acier a été utilisé pour la cheminée ouverte.

Un portal en la naturaleza

Casa de madera con formas orgánicas

Esta casa fue concebida como sencilla cabaña en la naturaleza. Un gran portal de vidrio que se puede pivotar hacia arriba, abre la sala de estar a todo lo ancho y enmarca la vista de la montaña. Siguiendo el ejemplo de las viviendas sencillas de la región, se usaron materiales de fabricación industrial: paredes de bloques de hormigón, el piso de la sala de estar es de hormigón liso, simples perfiles de acero como marcos de ventana y soportes de techo, mientras que un segmento de tubo de acero se transformó en chimenea abierta.

+1

0

Somerniemi, FI
Huttunen Lipasti Architects
2002, 120 m²

At Home in the Forest

Wood-Frame Hillside House

The cabin is located in a wood between open meadows and a lake. The buildings are sited along a pathway that winds through birch trees. This path begins on the edge of the meadow and leads through the villa, to the sauna and lakeshore. The black stain finish of the timber buildings reinterprets the dark tone of the pine forest. The building opens towards the lake and is almost totally enclosed toward the meadow. The site was left in its natural state. The birch foliage shades the interior from harsh sunlight in the summer. The heat-storing fireplace and bathrooms are organised about the central masonry wall.

Im Wald zu Hause

Holzhaus am Seehang

Die pavillonartige Hausanlage liegt im Wald zwischen offenen Weiden und einem See. Die Bauten liegen entlang eines Pfades, der am Weidenrand beginnt und durch das Haus, zur Sauna und weiter zum Seeufer führt. Die schwarz gebeizte Holzschalung setzt den dunklen Ton des Kieferwalds in der Architektur fort. Der Bau öffnet sich zum See hin und verschließt sich zu den Weiden auf der Rückseite. Der Bauplatz wurde im natürlichen Zustand belassen. Das Laub der Birken schützt die Innenräume vor Überhitzung durch die Sommersonne. Ein Kamin und die Badezimmer wurden um eine zentrale Massivmauer vorgesehen.

Avoir la forêt pour maison

Maison en bois à flanc de colline

La maison pavillonnaire est située dans une forêt, entre champs et lac. La construction se trouve le long d'un chemin, qui démarre à la limite d'un champ et se poursuit le long de la maison jusqu'au sauna, puis jusqu'au bord du lac. Le coffrage en bois teinté noir s'harmonise avec le ton sombre de la forêt de pins. La construction s'ouvre sur le lac et est fermée à l'arrière, du côté des champs. Le site a été laissé dans son état naturel. Le feuillage des bouleaux protège les pièces intérieures de la chaleur du soleil estival. Une cheminée et les salles de bains ont été prévues autour d'un pan de mur central.

Hogar en el bosque

Casa de madera junto al lago

Esta casa tipo pabellón está emplazada en el bosque entre pastizales y un lago. La construcción se extiende por un sendero que comienza junto a los pastizales y conduce a través de la casa hacia el sauna y más allá a la orilla de lago. El color negro del revestimiento de madera incorpora el tono oscuro del bosque a la arquitectura. La construcción se abre hacia el lago, mientras que permanece cerrada hacia los pastizales. Los abedules protegen el interior contra el sol de verano. Los cuartos de baño y una chimenea se ubicaron en torno a una pared central.

All-Wood House

Forest Refuge on a Lakeshore

Finland's extensive forests make wood a readily and affordably available material for house construction there. The architect heads a Faculty for Wood Construction in Helsinki, is specialized in this most Finnish of all materials, and explored its potential in various capacities on this house. White-stained and clear-varnished pine boards set the scene in the light-filled interiors. The grey-stained wooden exterior cladding creates a contrast to the light tones of the interiors and blends well with the earthen hues of the surrounding forest. The covered wooden deck shelters the entrance and serves as a comfortable terrace in the midst of the Nordic forest.

Komplett aus Holz

Waldrefugium am Seerand

Dank der großen Waldflächen steht das Material Holz in Finnland kostengünstig für den Hausbau zur Verfügung. Der Architekt, Inhaber eines Lehrstuhls für Holzbauweise in Helsinki, hat sich diesem Baustoff intensiv gewidmet und ihn bei diesem Haus auf vielfältige Weise eingesetzt. Weiß lasierte und mit Klarlack versiegelte Kieferbretter wurden an den Wänden und Böden im hellen Inneren vorgesehen. Die grau lasierten Außenwände stehen dazu im Kontrast und fügen sich in die Farbtöne des umgebenden Waldes ein. Das überdachte Holzdeck schützt den Eingang und dient als Freiterrasse inmitten des nordischen Waldes.

Maison tout en bois

Un refuge forestier au bord du lac

Grâce aux immenses forêts de Finlande, le bois de construction est disponible à moindre coût. L'architecte, qui occupe une chaire à Helsinki relative à la construction en bois, s'est entièrement consacré à ce matériau et l'a utilisé de manière originale et variée dans cette maison. Des planches de pin revêtues de lasure blanc et d'un vernis brillant ont été utilisées pour les murs et les planchers de l'intérieur. Les murs extérieurs, à lasure gris, apportent un contraste intéressant et se fondent aux tons du paysage forestier environnant. Le ponton en bois couvert protège l'entrée et sert de terrasse de plein air au cœur de la forêt nordique.

Toda de madera

Refugio en el bosque

Debido a las extensas zonas de bosque existentes, la madera es un material de construcción económico en Finlandia. El arquitecto, titular de una cátedra para arquitectura en madera en Helsinki, se ha dedicado de modo intensivo a este material, usándolo de diversas formas en esta casa. Para las paredes y pisos en el interior se usaron tablas de pino barnizadas en blanco y selladas con laca transparente. Las paredes exteriores barnizadas en gris se adaptan a los tonos de color del bosque circundante. El entarimado techado protege la entrada y sirve como terraza al aire libre.

Mikkeli, FI, Pekka Heikkinen, 2004, 80 m²

Pavilion under the Trees
Lakeside Country Residence

This house located on a large lake in rural Montana is both the hub of daytime activities at the site and a quiet retreat. The pristine site called for a sensitive intervention that respects the natural setting and the rugged climate with its seasonal extremes. The house stretches from a rock ledge to a wetland of cattails. A linear wall plane with a rusted, weathering steel skin slices through the site. Wood-clad boxes containing bathrooms lie to the north. The living spaces to the south extend onto a house-long wood deck. Tall walls of glass with operable panels emphasize the dramatic lake view here.

Pavillon unter Bäumen
Landhaus am See
Dieses an einem großen See im ländlichen Montana gelegene Haus dient zugleich als aktives Zentrum und Refugium. Die unberührte Landschaft und die klimatischen Extreme forderten einen sensiblen Umgang. Der Bau erstreckt sich zwischen einem Felsrücken und einem Biotop. Die Funktionsbereiche werden entlang einer das Grundstück durchschneidenden Wandscheibe angeordnet. Mit Holz eingeschalte Badezimmerkisten sind nach Norden, die Wohnbereiche nach Süden zum hauslangen Holzdeck orientiert. Hohe Glaswände mit Schiebeelementen betonen die freie Aussicht auf See und Berge.

Pavillon sous les arbres
Maison de campagne lacustre
Cette maison, située au bord d'un grand lac dans la campagne du Montana, est à la fois un lieu d'activités dynamique et un refuge. La nature vierge et le climat variable ont rendu les travaux délicats. La construction s'étend entre le dos d'une paroi rocheuse et un biotope. Les pièces fonctionnelles ont été placées le long d'un mur qui traverse le terrain. Les salles de bains, habillées de bois, sont orientées vers le nord, les pièces à vivre sont plein sud et donnent sur la terrasse en bois de la largeur de la maison. De hautes baies vitrées coulissantes magnifient la vue sur le lac et les montagnes.

Pabellón bajo árboles
Casa de campo junto al lago
Esta casa ubicada a orillas de un gran lago en una zona rural de Montana sirve al mismo tiempo como centro activo y refugio. El paisaje virgen y los extremos climáticos exigieron un manejo sensible. La construcción se extiende entre una loma de rocas y un biótopo. Las áreas funcionales se distribuyen a lo largo de una placa de pared que atraviesa el terreno. Los baños encajonados en madera están orientados hacia el norte, mientras que las áreas de habitación se orientan hacia la alargada cubierta de madera al sur. Las altas paredes de vidrio con elementos corredizos visibles realzan la vista dramática sobre el lago y las montañas.

Rural Montana, USA, Bohlin Cywinski Jackson, 2002, 175 m²

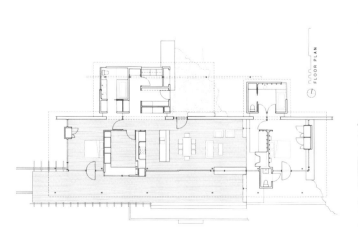

FLOOR PLAN

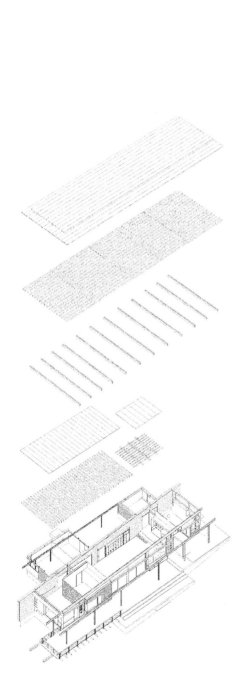

Canadian Spirit

House Group at Lake Erie

The program for this house was deployed in three interconnected building volumes that form an intimate entrance courtyard from which all three wings are accessed. The floor plan reflects the specific needs of the clients. Since no children are present, a small kitchen was deemed sufficient in order to create a generous living room with a gallery that opens to the bedroom on the upper level of the lakeside main house wing. Canadian granite was used to create lively interior and exterior wall surfaces. Cedar, galvanized tin, and glass complete the harmonious selection of materials.

Kanadischer Geist

Hausgruppe am Eriesee

Die Funktionen des Hauses wurden in drei miteinander verbundenen Baukörpern untergebracht. Diese definieren einen intimen Eingangshof, von dem aus das zum See hin gelegene Haupthaus betreten wird. Das Raumangebot entspricht den speziellen Bedürfnissen des kinderlosen Besitzerpaars: die recht kleine Küche ist abgeschlossen, der Wohn-Essraum wurde dafür großzügig mit einer offenen Galerie zum Schlafzimmer im OG gestaltet. Kanadischer Granit erzeugt stimmungsvolle Wandflächen innen und außen. Cedarholz, Zinkblech und Glas komplettieren die harmonisch abgestimmte Materialienpalette.

Ontario, Canada, EFM Design, 2002, 380 m²

L'esprit canadien

Maison au bord du lac Erié

Les pièces fonctionnelles de la maison ont été disposées dans trois éléments de construction reliés entre eux. Ces derniers forment une cour intime, où l'on pénètre par le corps de bâtiment principal, situé le long du lac. L'espace répond aux besoins spécifiques du couple de propriétaires sans enfants : la petite cuisine est fermée, le salon-salle à manger, au contraire, a été conçu de manière généreuse et s'ouvre sur l'étage supérieur par une galerie conduisant à la chambre à coucher. Le granit canadien compose d'originales surfaces murales, à l'intérieur comme à l'extérieur. Le bois de cèdre, la feuille de zinc et le verre complètent cette harmonieuse palette de matériaux.

Espíritu canadiense

Residencia junto al lago Erie

Las áreas funcionales de la casa se distribuyeron en tres cuerpos constructivos interconectados. Éstos definen un patio de entrada, desde el cual se entra a la casa principal orientada hacia el lago. El espacio disponible corresponde a las necesidades específicas de los propietarios, una pareja sin niños: la cocina bastante pequeña está aislada, mientras que el área de comedor y sala de estar se configura generosamente con una galería abierta hacia el dormitorio en el piso superior. El granito canadiense crea un ambiente particular en el interior y el exterior. Madera de cedro, chapa de cinc y vidrio completan la gama de materiales armónicamente seleccionados.

+1

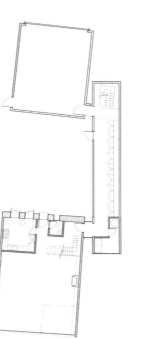

0

Mercer Island, WA, USA
The Miller / Hull Partnership
2003, 390 m²

House with a Bridge

Lakeside Residence on Three Levels

Located between a forest and sweeping lake vistas, this house is entered from the rooftop on the third floor. A bridge spans from the adjacent slope through the forest to the covered roof terrace. A central stair descends to the living area on the ground floor that opens to the shore. As one descends, the view alternates between open water and forested hill side. The house functions are contained in two cantilevered box forms with the private spaces on the second and third floor and a self contained guest house on the top floor. The „boxes" are clad on all surfaces in clear cedar siding that continues inside on the ceilings.

Haus mit Brücke

Haus am See auf drei Ebenen

Dieses zwischen Wald und See gelegene Haus wird über eine Dachterrasse betreten. Eine Brücke spannt sich vom dem gegenüberliegenden Hang zur überdachten Dachterrasse. Eine zentrale Treppe führt herunter zum Wohnbereich im EG, der sich zum Strand hin öffnet. Beim Durchschreiten der Treppe wechselt der Ausblick zwischen Wald- und Seeseite. Die Wohnräume sind in zwei „Holzkisten" untergebracht. Private Zimmer befinden sich in den OG's. Eine Gästesuite genießt die besondere Lage auf der Dachebene. Die „Kisten" sind rundum, sogar im Inneren auf den Deckenunterseiten, mit Cedarholz eingeschalt.

Maison avec ponton

Résidence lacustre sur trois étages

Cette maison, située entre une forêt et des paysages
lacustres à perte de vue, a sa porte d'entrée sur une
terrasse de toit. Un ponton se dresse entre le pente
opposée à la maison et la terrasse de toit couverte.
Un escalier central conduit au rez-de-chaussée de
l'habitation, qui s'ouvre sur la plage. En descendant
l'escalier, on alterne entre vue sur la forêt et vue sur le
lac. Les pièces à vivre sont réparties entre deux espaces
dits « caisses de bois ». Les chambres se trouvent aux
étages supérieurs. Une suite pour les invités jouit
quant à elle d'une situation privilégiée sous les toits.
Les espaces, dits « caisses », sont recouverts de bois de
cèdre, y compris le plafond intérieur.

Casa con puente

Casa lacustre de tres plantas

A esta casa, ubicada entre un bosque y amplias vistas
lacustres, se entra a través de una azotea. Un puente
conecta el acantilado situado enfrente con esta terraza
techada. Una escalera central desciende al área de
habitación en la planta baja, que a su vez se abre hacia
la playa. Cuando se transita por la escalera, la vista se
alterna entre el lado del bosque y el lado del lago. Las
habitaciones se encuentran alojadas en dos especies
de „cajas de madera". Las habitaciones privadas están
en los pisos superiores. Hay una suite para huéspedes
en el nivel del techo. Dichas „cajas" están revestidas
completamente con madera de cedro, incluyendo el
interior y los lados inferiores de los techos.

Rural NY, USA
Bohlen Cywinski Jackson
2004, 400 m²

Linearity on the Lake
Forest Home in New York State
This vacation house will later be a full time residence. The linear plan enhances lake views while the low roof profile and stained green exterior cedar siding meld into the surrounding forest. From the entry, one is drawn in by the extraordinary view through the house to the Adirondack Mountains beyond. All major rooms have a view of the lake. The living room, dining room and kitchen flow into each other to create a seamless living space. Adjacent to the living room, the master bedroom opens onto a deck with views through the forest to a secluded cove. The upper level accommodates two bedrooms and a recreation area for guests.

Wohnschiene am See
Waldhaus in New York State
Dieses Ferienhaus wird später das Hauptdomizil der Bauherrschaft. Der lineare Plan betont die Ausblicke auf den See, während das geduckte Dachprofil und die grün gebeizten Holzfassaden sich sensibel in den Wald einfügen. Vom Eingang aus öffnet sich ein Blick durch das Haus auf die Adriondack Berge dahinter. Die Haupträume sind alle mit Seeblick angelegt. Die Wohn-, Ess- und Kochbereiche werden zu einem locker miteinander verbundenen Raumgefüge zusammengeführt. Das Elternschlafzimmer daneben öffnet sich zu einem Holzdeck mit Wald- und Seeblick. Das Obergeschoss beherbergt zwei Schlafzimmer und einen Gästebereich.

Vivre au bord d'un lac
Maison forestière dans l'Etat de New York
Cette maison de villégiature deviendra plus tard la résidence principale de son maître d'ouvrage. Le plan linéaire met en valeur les vues sur le lac, tandis que le toit abaissé et les façades en bois teinté vert se fondent à l'environnement forestier. L'entrée offre une perspective à travers toute la maison sur le mont Adriondack situé à l'arrière. Les pièces principales donnent toutes sur le lac. Le salon, la salle à manger et la cuisine communiquent pour former un espace convivial et aéré. La chambre à coucher des parents s'ouvre sur une terrasse en bois avec vue sur la forêt et sur le lac. L'étage supérieur abrite deux chambres à coucher et une pièce pour les invités.

Linealidad junto al lago
Casa de bosque en el Estado de Nueva York
Esta casa vacacional será el domicilio principal de sus dueños. El plano lineal realza las vistas sobre el lago, mientras que el perfil bajo del techo y las verdes fachadas de madera se integran al bosque. Desde la entrada se abre una vista a través de la casa sobre las montañas de Adirondack al fondo. Las habitaciones principales tienen vista al lago. Las áreas de estar, comedor y cocina se congregan con soltura. El dormitorio principal adyacente tiene vista al bosque y al lago. El piso superior alberga dos dormitorios y un área para huéspedes.

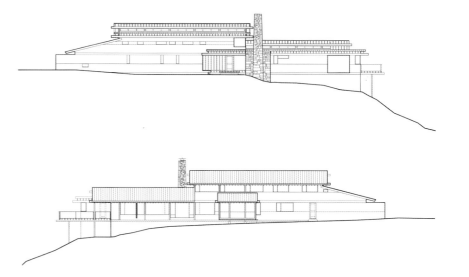

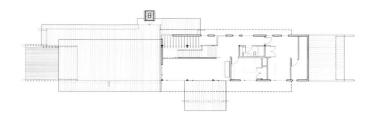

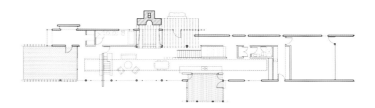

Curvature at the Entrance

Lakeside Residence near Seattle

This wooden-clad, rectilinear residential ensemble stretches elegantly along the lakeshore. Its orthogonal rhythms are syncopated by a metal-sheathed wall element that curves out to mark the entrance and spatially enriches the living room inside. During daytime natural light enters the skylight from above to create an almost sacred, church-like ambience. At night, artificial lighting from above transforms it into a tower of light. The Classic Modern furniture pieces chosen all radiate the same warm, comfortable feeling that imbues the interior and exterior materials – wood, stone, and glass.

Kurve am Eingang

Wohnsitz am See bei Seattle

Das Hausensemble aus rechtwinkeligen, mit Holz verkleideten Baukörpern erstreckt sich elegant entlang des Seeufers. Die Rechtwinkligkeit der Volumen wird durch die markante metallene Kurve der Eingangsscheibe unterbrochen. Diese setzt sich in der Wohnhalle im Inneren fort, wo bei Tag natürliches Licht und nachts künstliche Beleuchtung von oben in den hohen Raum geführt wird. Bei den Möbeln entschied man sich für Klassiker des modernen Designs, die jedoch allesamt von derselben warmen Wohnlichkeit gekennzeichnet sind, die auch die eleganten Innen- und Außenmaterialien - Holz, Stein und Glas - ausstrahlen.

Une entrée tout en courbe

Résidence lacustre proche de Seattle

La demeure, constituée d'éléments de construction rectangulaires et revêtus de bois, s'étire élégamment au bord du lac. Les volumes anguleux de la maison sont adoucis par la courbure prononcée de la vitre d'entrée. Celle-ci se prolonge à l'intérieur jusqu'au cœur de la maison – la lumière du jour inonde par le haut cette vaste pièce, du matin au soir, et un éclairage artificiel l'éclaire la nuit. Des meubles classiques, d'un design moderne, ont été choisis pour équiper la maison : ils lui donnent un confort chaleureux et accueillant. Les riches matériaux utilisés à l'intérieur et à l'extérieur, comme par exemple le bois, la pierre et le verre, offrent également un standing certain.

Curva en la entrada

Casa lacustre cerca de Seattle

El conjunto residencial formado por cuerpos constructivos rectangulares, revestidos de madera, se extiende con elegancia por la orilla del lago. El carácter rectangular de los volúmenes se ve interrumpido por la marcada curva metálica de la entrada. La misma se prolonga en el interior del área de estar, cuyo alto espacio se ilumina durante el día con luz natural y por la noche con luz artificial. Para los muebles se optó por clásicos del diseño moderno que exhalan la misma acogedora calidez como los materiales empleados: madera, piedra y vidrio.

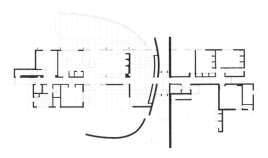

Seattle, WA, USA, Olson Kundberg Kundig Allen, 2004, 465 m²

The Architects. Photo Credits.
Die Architekten. Les architectes. Los arquitectos.
Bildnachweis. Crédits photographiques. Créditos fotograáficos.

12
Villa Nina, Kustavi, Finland
Kimmö Köpilä, Turku, Finland
Topi Laaksonen, Tampere, Finland
kimmo.kopila@oleron.fi
topi.laaksonen@elisanet.fi
Photos: page 12-15 Hans Koistinen
page 14-15 Tommi Grönlund

26
Ocean Boulevard House, Longboat Key, Florida, USA
Guy Peterson/OFA, Inc.
Sarasota, Florida, USA
www.guypeterson.com
mail@guypeterson.com
Photos: Steven Brooke Studios

16
Juquehy Beach House, Sao Sebastio, BR
Puntoni Arquitetos
São Paulo, Brazil
www.puntoni.arq.br
alvaro@puntoni.arq.br
Photos: Nelson Kon

30
Casa Felix, Ubatuba, Brazil
Anne Marie Sumner
São Paulo, SP, Brazil
ams-arquitetura@uol.com.br
Photos: pages 10-11, 30-33 Nelson Kon

18
Weekend House, Barra do Sahy, Brazil
Nitsche Aquitetetos Associados
São Paulo, Brazil
lua@nitsche.com.br
Photos: Nelson Kon

34
Mediterranean House, Ibiza, Spain
Ramon Esteve Estudio de Arquitectura
Valencia, Spain
www.ramonesteve.com
estudio@ramonesteve.com
Photos: page 34-37, 176 Ramon Esteve

22
Dune House, Ofir, Portugal
José Fernando Goncalves; Christina Guedes
Porto, Portugal
www.menosemais.com
josefgoncalves@sapo.pt
guedes.decampos@sapo.pt
Photos: Alessandra Chemollo

38
Tropical House, Bahia, Brazil
Fabrizio Ceccarelli
Rio de Janiero, Brazil
diretoria@a3assessoria.com
Photos: Otto Weisser

42
Guaecá Beach House, São Sebastião, Brazil
Mario Biselli
São Paulo, Brazil
www.bkweb.com.br
biselli@bkweb.com.br
Photos: Nelson Kon

58
Island House, Guemes Island, WA, USA
The Miller/Hull Partnership
Seattle, Washington, USA
www.millerhull.com
esilva@millerhull.com
Photos: John Dimaio

46
Siesta Key House, Florida, USA
Guy Peterson/OFA, Inc.
Sarasota, Florida, USA
www.guypeterson.com
mail@guypeterson.com
Photos: Steven Brooke Studios

60
Coastal Home, San Juan Island, WA, USA
Suyama Peterson Deguchi
Seattle, Washington, USA
www.suyamapetersondeguchi.com
info@suyamapetersondeguchi.com
Photos: Paul Warchol

48
Casa in Lagoa de Uruaú, Beberibe, Brazil
Gerson Castelo Branco
Fortaleza, Ceará, Brazil
www.gersoncastelobranco.com.br
paraqueira@yahoo.com.br
Photos: Tadeu Lubambo

62
Decatur Island Residence, WA, USA
Suyama Peterson Deguchi
Seattle, Washington, USA
www.suyamapetersondeguchi.com
info@suyamapetersondeguchi.com
www.suyamapetersondeguchi.com
info@suyamapetersondeguchi.com
Photos: Paul Warchol

54
Bach House, Coromandel Peninsula,
New Zealand
Crosson Clarke Carnachan Architects
Auckland. New Zealand
architects@ccsaa.co.nz
Photos: Cover, pages 54-57
Patrick Reynolds

64
M-House, Cañete, Peru
Barclay & Crousse architecture
Paris, France
www.barclaycrousse.com
atelier@barclaycrousse.com
Photos: Jean Pierre Crousse

68
Casa Equis, Cañete, Peru
Barclay & Crousse architecture
Paris, France
www.barclaycrousse.com
atelier@barclaycrousse.com
Photos: cover, page 68-71, Jean Pierre Crousse

84
Stinson Beach House, California, USA
Turnbull Griffin Haesloop Architects
Berkeley, California, USA
http://www.tgharchs.com
info@tgharchs.com
Photos: page 84-85, 87,
Matthew Millman,
page 86, 86-87 Proctor Jones Jr.

72
Rose House, Kiama, Australia
Engelen Moore Architects
Sydney, Australia
www.engelenmoore.com.au
architects@engelenmoore.com.au
Photos: Ross Honeysett

88
Horizon House, Atami, Shizuoka, Japan
Shinichi Ogawa & Associates
Tokyo / Hiroshima, Japan
www.shinichiogawa.com
info@shinichiogawa.com
Photos: Nacása & Partners Inc., Koichi Torimura

76
Casa Poli, Coliumo, Chile
Pezo von Ellrichhausen
Concepción, Chile
www.pezo.cl
m_pezo@yahoo.es
Photos: pages 52-53, 76-79 Cristobal Palma

92
Normandy Park Home, Washington, USA
Balance Associates Architects
Seattle, Washington, USA
balanceassociates.com
tom@balarc.com
Photos: Lindsay Photo Design

80
Wetland House, Port Hadlock, WA, USA
Eggleston Farkas Architects
Seattle, Washington, USA
www.eggfarkarch.com
office@eggfarkarch.com
Photos: Jim Van Gundy

94
Panorama House, Mornington Peninsula, Australia
SJB Architects
Southbank, Victoria, Australia
www.sjb.com.au
architects@sjb.com.au
Photos: Peter Hyatt + Tony Miller

98
Flinders House, Victoria, Australia
Jackson Clements Burrows Pty Ltd Architects
Melbourne, Australia
www.jcba.com.au
jacksonclementsburrows@jcba.com.au
Photos: Emma Cross, Gollings Photography

108
Mussel Shoals House, Ventura, California, USA
Design ARC Architects
Los Angeles, California, USA
www.designarc.net
dmccarthy@designarc.net
Photos: Fotoworks Benny Chan

100
Vertical House, Venice Beach, California, USA
Lorcan O'Herlihy
Los Angeles, California, USA
www.loharchitects.com
loh@loharchitects.com
Photos: Michael Wechsler Photography

112
Bayside House, Bay of Islands, New Zealand
Pete Bossley Architects Ltd
Auckland, New Zealand
www.bossleyarchitects.co.nz
pete@bossleyarchitects.co.nz
Photos: page 2-3, 112-115 Patrick Reynolds

102
Seola Beach House, Burien, Washington, USA
Eggleston Farkas Architects
Seattle, Washington, USA
www.eggfarkarch.com
office@eggfarkarch.com
Photos: Jim Van Gundy

116
Knight House, Newport Beach, CA, USA
Abramson Teiger Architects
Culver City, California, USA
www.abramsonteiger.com
trevor@abramsonteiger.com
Photos: Bill Timmerman

106
Malibu Beach House, Malibu, California, USA
Shubin + Donaldson Architects
Culver City, California, USA
www.shubinanddonaldson.com
rshubin@sandarc.com
Photos: Tom Bonner

118
Feinstein House, Malibu, California, USA
Kanner Architects
Los Angeles California, USA
www.kannerarch.com
shkanner@kannerarch.com
Photos: John Linden

122
Manhattan Beach, California, USA
Design ARC Architects
Los Angeles, California, USA
www.designarc.net
info@designarc.net
Photos: Erhard Pfeiffer

134
Taplin House, Adelaide, Australia
Con Bastiras Architect
Kings Park, SA, Australia
bastiras@internode.on.net
Photos: page 128-129, 134-135 Trevor Fox

124
Semiahmoo House, Semiahmoo, WA, USA
Finne Architects, Nils C. Finne, AIA
Seattle, Washngton, USA
www.finne.com
nils@finne.com
Photos: Art Grice

136
Burraworrin House, Flinders, Australia
Gregory Burgess Pty Ltd Architects
Richmond, Australia
www.gregoryburgessarchitects.com.au
gba@gregoryburgessarchitects.com.au
Photos: Trevor Mein

126
Treasure Home, Bainbridge Island, WA, USA
The Miller/Hull Partnership
Seattle, Washington, USA
www.millerhull.com
esilva@millerhull.com
Photos: Nic Lehoux

140
Lakeside House, Berlin, Germany
Nägeli Architekten
Berlin, Germany
www.naegeliarchitekten.de
buero@naegeliarchitekten.de
Photos: page 138-143 Ulrich Schwarz, Berlin

130
Hover House, Dawesville, Australia
Iredale Pedersen Hook Architects
Perth, Australia
ipharchs@iinet.net.au
Photos: page 130-132 Tony Nathan
page 133 Adrian Iredale

144
Chicken Point House, Idaho, USA
Olson Sundberg Kundig Allen Architects
Seattle, Washington, USA
www.olsonsundberg.com
Photos: Benjamin Benschneider

148
Country House, Somerniemi, Finland
Huttunen & Lipasti Architects
Helsinki, Finland
www.huttunen-lipasti.fi
risto.huttunen@huttunen-lipasti.fi
Photos: Marko Huttunen

162
Galloway House, Mercer Island, WA, USA
The Miller/Hull Partnership
Seattle, Washington, USA
www.millerhull.com
esilva@millerhull.com
Photos: Benjamin Benschneider

152
Wood House, Mikkeli, Finland
Pekka Heikkinen
Helsinki, Finland
ark.6b@kolumbus.fi
Photos: Kimmo Räisänen

164
Shelving Rock House, New York State, USA
Bohlin Cywinski Jackson
Wilkes-Barre, Pennsylvania, USA
www.bcj.com
pbohlin@bcj.com
Photos: Nic Lehoux

154
Point House, Montana, USA
Bohlin Cywinski Jackson
Seattle, Washington, USA
www.bcj.com
smongillo@bcj.com
Photos: Nic Lehoux

168
Lake Washington Home, Seattle, WA, USA
Olson Sundberg Kundig Allen Architects
Seattle, Washington, USA
www.olsonsundberg.com
Photos: Eduardo Calederon

158
Lake Erie Home, Ontario, Canada
EFM Design Emanuela Frattini Magnusson
New York, NY, USA
www.efmdesign.com
efm@efmdesign.com
Photos: Bill Whitaker

Casa Na Xemena, Ibiza, Spain
Ramon Esteve Estudio de Arquitectura, 2003, page 34